I Can't See
GOD
Because
I'm in
the Way

Bruce Bickel & Stan Jantz

HARVEST HOUSE PUBLISHERS

EUGENE, OREGON

Bruce Bickel: Published in association with the literary agency of Mark Sweeney & Associates, Bonita Springs, FL 34135.

Stan Jantz: Published in association with the literary agency of Mark Sweeney & Associates, Bonita Springs, FL 34135.

ConversantLife.com is a registered trademark of Conversant Media Group. Harvest House Publishers, Inc., is a licensee of the federally registered trademark ConversantLife.com.

Cover by Abris, Veneta, Oregon

Cover photo © DrGrounds / iStockphoto

I CAN'T SEE GOD...BECAUSE I'M IN THE WAY
Copyright © 2009 by Bruce Bickel and Stan Jantz
Published by Harvest House Publishers
Eugene, Oregon 97402
www.harvesthousepublishers.com

Library of Congress Cataloging-in-Publication Data

Bickel, Bruce
I can't see God—because I'm in the way / Bruce Bickel and Stan Jantz.
p. cm.
ISBN 978-0-7369-2619-5 (pbk.)
1. Spirituality. 2. Spiritual life—Christianity. 3. Christian life. I. Jantz, Stan II. Title.
BV4501.3.B483 2009
248.4—dc22

2009001237

Printed in the United States of America

09 10 11 12 13 14 15 16 / VP-NI / 10 9 8 7 6 5 4 3 2 1

Download a Deeper Experience

Bruce Bickel and Stan Jantz are part of a faith-based online community called ConversantLife.com. At this website, people engage their faith in entertainment, creative arts, science and technology, global concerns, and other culturally relevant topics. While you're reading this book, or after you have finished reading, go to www.conversantlife .com/brucebickel and www.conversantlife.com/stanjantz and use these icons to read and download additional material from Bruce and Stan that is related to the book.

Resources: Download study guide materials for personal devotions or a small-group Bible study.

Videos: Click on this icon for interviews with Bruce and Stan and video clips on various topics.

Blogs: Read through Bruce and Stan's blogs and articles and comment on them.

Podcasts: Stream ConversantLife.com podcasts and audio clips from Bruce and Stan.

conversant **life** .com

engage your faith

Contents

A Note from the Authors

We need to tell you two things at the outset. First, this book is a companion to our last book, *I'm Fine with God...It's Christians I Can't Stand.* In that book we went on a rant about how we're annoyed by hypocritical Christians whose conduct turns people away from considering Christ. In this book, we turn the focus (and criticism) inward.

Second, we're two guys who have been writing Christian books together for more than a decade. Our faith journeys have been pretty similar, and our books reflect lessons that we've both learned from God at roughly the same time. We each write separate portions of our books, but the guy who is writing usually speaks for both of us in a combined voice (referring to "we," just as in this sentence). But this book is different. It involves an introspective examination of our private spiritual lives that we've managed to avoid in our prior books. This book is much more personal than our others have been, and it is all about honest self-examination, so it seemed disingenuous to use the amorphous "we" any longer. Consequently, the guy who is writing the chapter (Bruce or Stan) uses "I" when referring to himself. (This system provides honest self-disclosure while still providing a 50/50 chance of anonymity depending upon your guess of which one of us wrote the chapter.)

Finally, we aren't presuming that you're guilty of the same self-centered worship we discovered in our own lives. But we think Christians' self-interest often distracts them from their focus on God. Our prayer is that these chapters will prompt you to get out of the way so God can accomplish his will in and through you.

Bruce Bickel
Stan Jantz

Introduction

Jesus said, "I am come that you might have life, and that it might be awesome" (John 10:10, paraphrase).

But my spiritual life isn't awesome. So either Jesus was lying, or I'm not living the Christian life the way it was designed.

I'm no seminary graduate, but I know a little bit about Jesus. Considering that he was the one who knew no sin,[1] I must rule out the possibility that Christ's statement in John 10:10 was a lie or even an evangelical exaggeration. That leaves me basking in a blinding glimpse of the obvious—that I'm the one who is solely responsible for the mediocrity that is my Christian life.

Searching for the Awesome Life

Don't get me wrong, especially not on the first page of this book. (We can leave disagreements and misunderstandings between us for later in the book, when correct answers are more obscure and factual circumstances are more convoluted.) As to the issue of the public perception of my Christian life, let me immodestly say that a casual observer wouldn't consider my spiritual life to be deficient. Just the opposite. Some (dare I say most?) would consider me a paragon among Christ followers. (Are you starting to suspect that my obsession with the public opinion of my Christianity is a big part of my problem? You're right, but keep reading because you need to know that I'm not proud of it.)

Although Christ doesn't have a checklist, most of his disciples do, and I rank fairly high on most of these pharisaical surveys: regular church attendance, member of the church board, small group leader, fairly regular daily devotions (weekends excepted), prayer before meals, tithing on my income (earning superspiritual points for tithing on gross income instead of just the net), and acknowledging my faith before my neighbors with Christ-themed yard decorations at Christmas. Pretty good, eh? And therein lies the problem.

By outwardly objective standards, I've got my spiritual life together. But on the inside, the part that only God and I know about, things aren't always so great. Oh, they aren't bad. In fact, most of the time my faith life is good. But it is not *awesome.* And I want it to be awesome because Christ promised it could be great. (More correctly, in John 10:10 he promised it could be "abundant," but that was when he was speaking in King James English. Apparently God's lexicon has been updated because "awesome" is the word I hear from the Holy Spirit in moments of his conviction and exhortation regarding what my spiritual life could be.)

Like many Christians, I was enthusiastic about my faith immediately following my conversion. But somewhere along the line, my relationship with Christ skidded into a religious rut. I didn't actually get lazy, because I was a "doer" for Christ (see the above-listed credentials on my pharisaical survey). But I lost my passion for Christ. My love for him was constant, but my passion for him waned.

Perhaps God Should Be a Little Bit More like My Wife

Losing passion is not an uncommon phenomenon. It happens in all kinds of relationships when the newness wears off and familiarity breeds indifference. The same thing has happened in my marriage from time to time. But my wife is quick to snap me out of it. She doesn't deserve a mundane marriage, and she'll let me know when she senses that I'm putting our relationship on autopilot. She usually initiates the conversation with a casual hint along the lines of, "Hey! You're ignoring me again. Snap out of it!" And from there she gets more lovingly direct by citing specific examples that I'd prefer not to memorialize in print. I'm always glad when she brings my relational lethargy to my attention, but I couldn't avoid the confrontations even if I tried. When you eat meals together and sleep next to each other, it's difficult to avoid these "what needs to be said" conversations. In fact, they are unavoidable if you are married to my wife.

Over the years, God hasn't been as confrontational with me as my wife has been. At least he hasn't been as obvious about it as she is. So it was easy to let my spiritual relationship languish over time. It needed to be revitalized occasionally as much as my marriage did, but ignoring God was easier than dodging my wife. Yes, I know the Bible tells me that God is omnipresent (everywhere at all times). Yet staring at my wife across the kitchen table and lying beside her in our bed made her presence *seem* more real. God is spirit, and even though I know he is there, I can pretty easily pretend he isn't. What I don't see, I don't have to deal with.

I Became What Neither God nor I Wanted

Nothing in life is as vacuous as spiritual mediocrity. God certainly isn't happy with it. As Jesus himself said, "Lukewarm Christians make me wanna puke."[2] (Okay, the translations use phrases like "spit you out of my mouth," but I think my paraphrase is theologically correct and culturally apropos.) But a mediocre Christian is exactly what I had become. I knew God was displeased with my attitude, and I wasn't happy with it either.

Despite outward appearances, I had fallen into the trap of living a life of religiosity. All form, little substance. All rules, regulations, and ritual; no vibrant relationship with Christ. I was ending up with a kind of faith that I didn't want, a kind of faith that I perceived was characteristic in so many people of my parents' generation, a kind of faith that focused on being with God in heaven for eternity but not having much fun with Christ while on earth. For me, this was an unfulfilling and unsatisfactory kind of faith. I was living a spiritually schizophrenic life—I appeared one way on the outside and felt completely the opposite on the inside. My only comfort in this duplicitous life was the knowledge that a lot of other Christians were faking it too.

Faking It for Christ's Sake

This is the great shameful secret of the Christian faith: On a personal and very private level, many of us have a faith that doesn't seem to be working. Oh, we know we have our eternal salvation in the bag, but our day-to-day spiritual life is unfulfilling. We're stuck smack-dab in the middle of a mundane, boring, and routine existence. Where is the awesome life that Jesus promised in John 10:10? Where's the passion? Where's the fervor? We want it, but we don't have it—and we can't seem to find it. But if people ask us about the condition of our spiritual lives, we say that things are going great.

Is this a lie? Of course it is. But we excuse it (and frequently repeat it) due to the extenuating circumstances. After all, we're mature Christians. If *we* can't get it right, who can? And if we told new Christians about our struggles in the faith, they might be discouraged to the point of renouncing their faith for one less daunting. And if we confessed our misgivings to pre-Christians, they might abandon their inquiries into Christianity before they got saved. As loyal (albeit passionless) followers of Christ, we abhor the notion of dissuading people from God's kingdom. So we keep quiet about our discontent and put on spiritually cheerful faces. After all, considering the sacrificial death of Christ on the cross for us, the least we can do for him is to fake it.

I Have Met the Enemy, and He Is Me

The time finally came when I didn't want to play the game any longer. I still wanted to be a Christian for sure, but I didn't want to pretend any longer that everything was good between God and me. Something needed to change. I didn't know what it was, but I knew the Holy Spirit was gnawing at me through discontent with my present spiritual condition. Through a tapestry of circumstances that only God could weave, I became friends with a group of passionate Christians who were living outside the rut. They weren't living their parents' kind of Christianity. They weren't willing to fake it. They had the real deal.

I started listening to the podcast sermons of Bible teachers like Mike Erre from Rock Harbor Church in Costa Mesa and Richard Dahlstrom from Bethany Community Church in Seattle. I was infected with the spiritual enthusiasm of the staff and faculty at Biola University and Westmont College. God was surrounding me with living proof that the awesome life promised by Christ truly existed this side of heaven.

I reapplied myself to the disciplines of spiritual formation in a new way, asking God to bring about change in my spiritual life. I could sense that I was approaching the launch to an epic adventure. I knew I needed to overcome obstacles. I just didn't anticipate that I would be the biggest one.

Here's what God has been patiently teaching me: Throughout my journey to know him better, I have been my own greatest enemy. As it turns out, I'm much more self-centered than I imagined (even though I started with the assumption that I was a high-achiever among egomaniacs, and I had already been trying to keep my self-centeredness in check). I hadn't realized that my self-absorption was tainting even my most sincere efforts to know and love God. Call it self-deception or self-sabotage. Call it self-interest, narcissism, or egocentricity. Call it whatever you want, but just don't call it Christianity. I had detoured myself down a faith path that included Christ, but I was choosing the direction more than I was following him. Although I would have argued vehemently with anyone who made the accusation, I was subconsciously formulating a faith that had me at the center. It impacted the way I prayed, the way I read the Bible, and the way I responded to what God was trying to accomplish in and through me.

The pages that follow are not intended to be a confessional, although they include some of that. The primary purpose of this book is to describe the biblical design for giving God the preeminence he deserves. I haven't included any stories of self-flagellation or self-deprecation as punishment for my spiritual self-centeredness (which might be a disappointment to those of you with voyeuristic inclinations). I wasn't forced by my church to scrape dried chewing gum off the bottom of the pews as penitence for my spiritual self-absorption. I'm still involved in the ministries and projects I have served in for years, but now my efforts are motivated by God's glory rather than my own résumé. I'm enjoying my life so much more now that my spiritual priorities have been tweaked. As it turns out, sometimes just a little fine-tuning is all that is required to move your spiritual life from mediocre to awesome.

...Because I Don't Know What He Looks Like

A kindergarten teacher was observing her students while they were drawing pictures. She occasionally walked around to see each child's artwork. As she got to one little girl who was working diligently, she asked what the drawing was.

The girl replied, "I'm drawing God."

The teacher paused and said, "But no one knows what God looks like."

Without missing a beat or looking up from her drawing, the girl replied, "They will in a minute."

Getting a mental picture of God is easy when you are deciding for yourself what he looks like. But here's the problem: The God we envision is likely to be far different from the God who really is. We better learn to discern the difference, or we're at risk of following an imaginary imposter.

Ready and Eager for a Spiritual Do-Over

New beginnings are great. That's why January 1 is so popular with people. We get to put the old year behind us (deleting from our memory all of last year's embarrassing screw-ups and humiliations) and start over with a clean slate. The new year will be better, and to make sure that it is, we implement a few resolutions for the new year (to which we strictly adhere through mid-February if we're lucky).

As Christians, we often take the same approach with our spiritual life. We want to start over every once in a while. If our faith gets a little off track, we rededicate ourselves to being better about it. We often start on January 1. We might commit to a daily Bible reading program designed to get us from Genesis through Revelation in 365 daily passages. But by mid-February, we're bogged down in Leviticus, reading about dissecting goat innards for altar sacrifices, and suddenly we're not so committed to reading God's Word every day or all the way through.

And so it is with other aspects of our Christian life: We set our sights on a daily devotional time, a better prayer life, or a cutback in our bad habits (which usually constitute *sin,* but "bad habits" appears to be the preferred politically correct terminology). Many aspects of our Christian life need improvement. We know it and God knows it, and we deeply desire to commit ourselves to making progress in these areas. So we start with good intentions, but before long we're back to where we started. Undaunted, we want to try again, committing to doing better next time. We want continual chances for spiritual do-overs. Amazingly, God agrees.

We customarily commence our new exercise programs, diets, and financial budgets on January 1. But our commitments (and recommitments) to spiritual-life disciplines aren't confined to the calendar. If our spiritual life goes awry in May, we're usually eager to reinstitute a meaningful relationship with Christ as soon as possible, and we don't want to defer doing so until January 1 rolls around. In other words, we know that losing ten pounds will require personal sacrifice, so we're willing to wait until New Year's Day for that one. But sensing more of God's presence in our lives is such a good thing—and it doesn't require abstaining from pizza—we want to get started right away. Spiritual motivation to get back on track with God isn't connected to a calendar. All it takes to get us spiritually psyched up is a powerful sermon, an emotionally charged set of worship songs, or better yet, the unadulterated influence of the Holy Spirit.

Maybe we shouldn't feel too bad about making up for lost ground in our spiritual journeys. Don't get me wrong. We shouldn't celebrate the fact that we have fallen away from the Lord when it happens. We should deeply regret it. But we can be excited about recommitting to the actions and attitudes that will reconnect us to Christ. First of all, the Bible tells us that we're in good company. The list of those who needed a spiritual do-over includes Moses, King David, and Peter. (Those guys were spiritual stalwarts. Too bad the thing I have in common with them is their flaws.) More importantly, however, when we begin a spiritual do-over, we're on the verge of revitalizing our Christian lives. Exciting things are about to happen. Personally, I'm always confident that I'll get closer to Christ than I have been in the recent past. I'm ready to experience God in a new and a better way. To put it succinctly, I'm excited to get started with the spiritual do-over because I'm going to taste Christ again for the very first time.[1]

Eager to Enter the Promised Land

When I think of spiritual do-overs, I'm reminded of the Israelites at the end of their 40-year desert wandering. Like me, they had a long history of God's provision in their lives and their own frequent bouts of unfaithfulness. They were just coming off a long dry spell in their spiritual journey. But they were about to put all of that behind them and enter the promised land, a place where they would experience a renewed relationship with their God and celebrate being in the center of his will. The long-awaited promise of a fulfilled spiritual life—dare I say an *awesome* spiritual life—was about to be realized.

The resemblance of my do-over situations to the promised-land scenario often leads me to read the book of Deuteronomy. When reading through the Old Testament, I usually skip from Exodus directly to Joshua because the intervening books of Leviticus, Numbers, and Deuteronomy are the biblical equivalent of tryptophan for me.[2] But in the context of a spiritual do-over, Deuteronomy is appropriate and relevant reading material. It is a collection of farewell addresses that Moses gave to the Israelites as he prepared to die and they prepared to cross the Jordan River into the promised land under the direction of their new leader, Joshua. So in a sense, the book of Deuteronomy contains the famous last words of Moses to the Israelites as they prepared to embark on one of the biggest spiritual do-overs the world has ever witnessed. I figure if God thought those words were good enough for the spiritually dim-witted Israelites, then those same words might be equally applicable to me.

Boiled down to its essence, Moses' advice to the Israelites at the verge of their spiritual do-over is simply this: "And you must love the LORD your God with all your heart, all your soul, and all your strength."[3]

Perhaps this isn't a surprise to you. After all, "God" is the answer to most spiritual quandaries. Yet this verse is always interesting and instructive to me. The core of Moses' advice is not about adhering to the orders of their new leader (Joshua). And he doesn't emphasize avoidance of the immorality of the Philistine culture. Rather, Moses says that loving God wholeheartedly is the key component of success for the Israelites as they embark on their divinely appointed spiritual do-over.

As we will see, this succinct directive to love God with all their heart, soul, and strength contains a lot of substance. It also conveys a lot of freedom. Moses is telling the Israelites, and me, that a spiritual do-over—even a colossal one—doesn't require a lot of religious hoopla. Getting your spiritual act together isn't primarily about following your pastor/priest or acting puritanical. You don't need to utter some mystical incantations as a prerequisite to purify your soul, and you don't need to endure a pentathlon of penitence to achieve acceptability before God. Rather, our ability to reengage our Christian faith is simply a matter of loving God. But unlike the past, when our love was halfhearted, our new spiritual do-over will be successful because our love for God *this time* is wholehearted.

Jesus Agreed with Moses

If you don't find Moses' sermons to the Israelites to be particularly relevant or persuasive, let's shift to Jesus' teachings. But don't expect to find a different outcome. Like Moses, Jesus was a proponent of this "wholehearted love for God" concept. In fact, Christ would apply this spiritual principle not only to do-overs but also to our entire faith. He used a parable to explain: "The Kingdom of Heaven is like a treasure that a man discovered hidden in a field. In his excitement, he hid it again and sold everything he owned to get enough money to buy the field."[4]

A little backstory might help with this parable. In the first century AD, safe-deposit boxes hadn't been invented yet. And even if they existed, they would have been useless because you wouldn't have a bank branch in your neighborhood. And you couldn't hide your valuables in your house because home security systems consisted of nothing more than a goat at the doorway. So people used to bury their stash (meaning cash and jewelry, not drugs) in the ground. If this was you, then you wanted to make sure you owned the ground or at least had a leasehold interest, because whoever had a right to use the ground had the ownership rights to whatever was buried there.

You're probably thinking, *Well, if I hid my treasure in the ground,*

I would take it out of the ground before I sold the property. That's what most people did, but they also tended to keep the existence of the buried treasure a secret. Burying a treasure doesn't work very well if everybody knows about it. And when a person with a secret stash died unexpectedly because of a plague or a fatal oxcart collision, his secret died with him. That's apparently what happened in the prelude to Christ's parable.

When the story starts, we find an unassuming pedestrian taking a shortcut across a field. He stumbles on a small protrusion in the ground, and his curiosity pays off when he digs down and uncovers a buried treasure box containing valuables of unimaginable wealth. This was no slow-thinking guy, so he immediately recognized a shrewd business opportunity. He ran into town and checked the county records to determine who owned the property. Then he struck a deal for the purchase of the property. The seller (oblivious to the existence of the buried treasure) demanded a high price because he could sense that the buyer was anxious. The price was so high, in fact, that the buyer was forced to sell everything he owned to be able to raise the cash for the purchase. But the price he paid was infinitesimal compared to the value of the treasure he obtained.

Christ's parable explains what it means to love God with all your heart, all your soul, and all your strength. It means being sold out to God. We should be eager to give him all we've got. Like the buyer of the field, we need to be willing to sacrifice everything we consider valuable in life in order to obtain a spiritual life of much greater worth. When compared to what a life with Christ can be, what we're holding on to is of little value. Our relatively small priorities, our selfish desires, and our deteriorating material possessions are all worthless when compared to a life of close fellowship with Christ. Devoting all of our time, energy, and resources to God—in other words, loving him wholeheartedly—is a small price to pay for the huge reward of intimate fellowship with God Almighty.

Putting the Principle into Practice

Moses' call to love God with all your heart, soul, and strength, and Jesus' invitation to be completely sold out for God, are exactly the kind of exhortations we need when we initiate a spiritual do-over. We should have this goal of a wholehearted love for God emblazoned in our frontal lobes if we are to keep from falling away from him as quickly and often as we have done in the past. And remembering the concept is the easy part. Implementing it is the challenge.

Apparently Moses was hip to the fact that loving God with all our heart, soul, and strength sounds easy but isn't. Accordingly, he elaborated on his thesis statement with several practical guidelines for spiritual living. For example, Moses told the Israelites that their love for God must include a healthy dose of fear: "You must fear the LORD your God."[5]

But Moses wasn't referring to dread and trepidation. He wasn't suggesting that we be terrified of God as if he were some kind of holy ogre. To the contrary, Moses used "fear" in the sense of respect and honor. He wants us to revere the Lord.

Fear of the Lord is a predicate to loving him. It's hard to love someone you don't respect, but love for someone you admire comes naturally. And there is more. Authentic reverence (fear) for God will mean that we desire to act and think in a manner that pleases him, so Moses added the following component to his description of what wholehearted love looks like: "Do what is right and good in the LORD's sight."[6]

Doing what pleases God isn't as difficult as it may seem. Initially we might think that we will have to struggle to resist the tug and pull of temptation. But just the opposite should be true. It makes sense and is fairly straightforward: If you truly love God and fear him, you'll *want* to do what pleases him. And you'll want to refrain from those activities and attitudes that offend him.

Here's the point Moses was getting at: Our realization of who

God is should be enough to compel our love and obedience. God doesn't demand it, like a feudal tyrant forcing allegiance from the peasantry, but he deserves it because of who he is. However, with all due respect to Moses, given my proclivity for falling away from God, I'm more concerned about the converse to his point: If our love and obedience continually short-circuits and requires repeated spiritual do-overs, something must be seriously out of whack.

I used to think that the problem was my love for God—that I didn't love him enough. But I've come to realize that my problem wasn't that I didn't know *how* to love but rather that I didn't really know *whom* to love. I was only loving and fearing part of God, not the whole of him. I was focused on the aspects of his character that put me at ease, and I intentionally overlooked the ones that made me uncomfortable. I'm beginning to realize that the attributes of God that I ignored are the very ones that I need to grasp more fully if I'm going to break the cycle of repeated spiritual do-overs.

You Can't Love God If You're Following an Impostor

After my daughter graduated from college, she moved to Nashville for a few years. After her stint in exciting Music City, she returned home to the more sedate Fresno for a few months before relocating to Seattle. While in Fresno, she lived close to our family home, and we kept bumping into each other at our neighborhood haunts. Many times we would see each other at the gym when our workout schedules overlapped. She always chided me for avoiding the treadmill, which happened to be her favorite exercise. I, on the other hand, preferred the weight machines (because I could exercise while sitting down).

My daughter was shocked when she entered the gym one day and saw me on the treadmill. She knew that the sweaty runner was me because of my standard workout apparel: white shoes, black shorts, white T-shirt, and grey baseball cap with my grey hair sticking out from underneath. As sort of a cardio initiation prank, she sneaked up behind me. Timing my strides perfectly, she hopped onto the treadmill. The running platforms on those treadmills are hardly long enough for one person, so you can image the close proximity of two people on the same treadmill, with four legs in synchronized motion. Expecting to surprise me, she then tapped me on my shoulder. I turned around, or at least the man who she thought was me turned around. Instead of me, he was apparently a very handsome guy who could have been my stunt double. My daughter was so startled that she stopped running, but the treadmill didn't stop, and she was hurled backward and fell on her anatomical cushion about six feet behind the treadmill. Under the glare of everyone in the immediate proximity, including my treadmilling twin brother from whom I must have been separated at birth, she exclaimed, "You aren't my father, and I'm not following you anymore." Immediately thereafter she fled from the gym in embarrassment, only to turn back one last time at the door to verify again that the man on the treadmill wasn't me.

In the spiritual realm, many of us are making the same mistake as my daughter. We're following an impostor god that looks like the real God in many respects. But the god we're following is a cheap knockoff of the real thing. As if we were assembling a Mr. Potato Head, we've conjured up this fake god with many traits of the real God, but we've conveniently omitted the parts of the real God that challenge us.

In my own case, I had an idea of God in my mind that was correct as far as it went. But my concept wasn't all of God. And if you are interested in only part of him, you are trivializing the rest of him. Thus, loving and revering God is impossible if you have only a selective image of him.

Know and Love the God Who Is, Not the God You Have Concocted

My tendency has always been to focus only on the characteristics of God that were pleasant and to ignore the aspects of his character that required more of me. I wish I had been doing this unconsciously, but I did it so often that I'm too guilty to attribute my offense to spiritual sleepwalking. In the final analysis, I knew what I was doing, but I didn't love God wholeheartedly, so I didn't change.

For me, thinking about God in general has always been easier when I picture Jesus in particular. After all, Jesus was the visible image of the invisible God.[7] I had an expansive portfolio of mental images of Jesus:

- *Bobblehead Jesus.* At times, my concept of Christ had him sitting on the shelf like a good-luck charm. He was there when I wanted to look at him. He was a good reminder of my faith, and he brought a lighthearted lift into an otherwise dreary day.

- *Action-figure Jesus.* I could call on this Jesus for help whenever I was in trouble. I could picture him swooping down out of the sky—his robe ruffling in the wind like Superman's cape—as he invaded human time and space to come to my rescue.

- *Baby Jesus.* I didn't reserve this nativity-scene image of Jesus just for Christmastime. I reflected on it whenever I needed a sense of tranquility. I ignored the reality that the baby Jesus probably cried a lot and that the manger setting was tainted with the stink of manure from the stable animals. (Those elements didn't enhance the tranquility I was after.)

- *Shroud of Turin Jesus.* This is the image I relied upon when I wanted to reflect on the mystical and metaphysical Jesus. Mystery and wonder are associated with the Shroud, and often I needed a little bit more of that in my faith.

- *Shepherd Jesus.* When facing the reality of my own going astray, I thought about Jesus as the shepherd, willing to leave the 99 for the sake of the one lost sheep.[8]

- *Soft and tender Jesus.* We've all been figuratively beat up at times. The worst kind of attack comes from other Christians. This is when we need a Jesus who came to the defense of those who were ridiculed by the religious establishment. We want him to treat us the way he treated the woman caught in adultery.[9] Her accusers in the religious hierarchy were sent away speechless, and Jesus showed love and forgiveness to the woman without a word of critical judgment.

- *Tough-guy Jesus.* A soft and tender Jesus is fine, but I don't want him to be namby-pamby. At times, I needed to know that my faith was placed in a God who can take a stand and protect me when the going gets tough. This is when I envisioned the Christ who can overturn the tables of the crooks in the Temple in an outrage of righteous indignation.[10]

As expansive and accurate as this list is, it isn't exhaustive. It includes accurate images of God's character, but it is limited to the ones I wanted to envision. Conspicuously missing are the images of God's character that make me uncomfortable. In particular, I intentionally chose to ignore two portraits of God:

- *The holy Jesus.* I don't want to be reminded that God is holy.[11] To say God is holy is to say he is separated from evil. If I admit that holiness is part of God character, then the charge of Moses to "do what is right and good in the LORD's sight" requires that I abstain from my favorite evil practices. Most of my evil stuff doesn't seem all that bad to me, but it sets off alarm bells when measured by God's holiness standard.

- *The suffering Jesus.* I don't want to be reminded about the pain and agony that Christ endured at Calvary. This is why I much prefer the Protestant cross to the Catholic crucifix. For the Protestants, the cross is empty—it's a cross with nice, clean, unencumbered lines. The Catholics, however, keep Jesus on the cross, usually slumped over from the torture he endured. I know it can be argued that the cross should be empty because Christ doesn't remain on the cross—he was buried and rose again. But if I picture only an empty cross in my mind, I can conveniently forget Christ's suffering and his sacrifice for my sin. To have an appropriate fear of God—a reverence for him that reflects the suffering at Calvary—I need a constant reminder of what Jesus endured on the cross. I need a constant reminder that my sin has a consequence that took Jesus to the cross. Only then will I be more inclined to refrain from it.

Over the years I've managed to conjure up a profile for God that minimizes the consequence of sin in my life. If my conceptualized god doesn't really object to sin, I don't need to worry about it. And that has been the problem. My sin didn't take me away from the god of my imagination, but it certainly disrupted my fellowship with the God who is—the God who cannot abide sin.

Sin Lingers

As it turns out, God is much more intolerant of sin than I am. He thinks it is a big deal. A very big deal. I, on the other hand, apparently have a much higher threshold of tolerance for it. At least this is the assessment I must make if I examine my track record. Intellectually and theologically, I know sin is bad. But evidence would suggest that I approach sin much like I deal with the unhealthy habit of eating potato chips—it is very pleasurable for the moment, so I give in to the urge more than I should, but I know that ultimately it is not beneficial for me, so I don't overindulge. In the perspective of all of life, I apparently think that a little sin—like a few potato chips—can't be too bad if taken only occasionally and in moderation.

I manage to stay away from the egregious (and publicly noticeable) sins. I prefer the incognito variety. That way my wife, kids, friends, and neighbors still consider me to be a good guy. As a result, a lot goes on in my head that isn't obvious to a casual observer. I'm an expert at losing my temper without causing any veins in my neck to throb noticeably. I'm quick at composing a snide and hateful remark without letting it slip out of my mouth. I can instantly flash a hand gesture at a driver who cuts me off on the freeway while managing to keep it obscured from the view of anyone riding in the shotgun seat. And as for my visits to the bookstore or the newsstands at the airport, I have developed extrasensory peripheral vision so I can stare at the sexually stimulating covers on the men's magazines while standing directly in front of the display section for business and finance periodicals. Other examples come to mind, but there is no need to get salacious in this discussion.

I'm not proud of this un-Christlike behavior, and I'd prefer to rid my life of it, but I allow it and live with it. And my guess is that you might be doing likewise, so we ought to be asking ourselves why. Why do we refrain from big sins but feel comfortable with lesser ones? I've been thinking about this question for a while, so allow me to postulate an answer that might be applicable for all of us. I think we assume that severe transgressions will have disastrous effects but that insignificant sins have little impact. Certainly that is true as far as legal ramifications are concerned. (Murder results in jail time, but you probably won't be incarcerated for flipping your middle finger at another driver.) But on a purely theological basis, this rule of proportionality between actions and consequences doesn't apply. All of our sins, regardless of how seemingly inconsequential, have a detrimental effect on our relationship with God.

If we were arrested for criminal conduct, I'm sure we'd be on our knees in the jail cell, praying for forgiveness. We would be faced with the stark reality that our behavior had broken our relationship with God, and we'd approach him with a reverent and repentant attitude. However, if our transgression is only a "little white lie," we think nothing of it, and we go on with life—including our spiritual life—as if nothing had happened. But the fact remains that we knowingly violated God's principles with any untruth, and we're arrogantly and presumptuously pretending that such an affront to God is of no consequence. We mistakenly think that we can sin and that God won't notice. But our sin doesn't dissipate into thin air without a residual effect.

I'm reminded of my first date with my wife. We met in college when I was a sophomore and she was a freshman. She was out of my league, but I noticed her on the first day she came to campus, and I put the moves on her before any other guy could get to her. I didn't have a lot going for me in those days, but I was driving a nice sports car. It was a BMW coupe. This was the vehicle that I parked in front of her dorm when I picked her up for our first date. In a display of courtesy (that has dissipated over the years of our marriage), I escorted her to the car and opened the passenger door for her and then closed it after she was seated. At that very moment, the excitement of the circumstances caused volcanic eruptions in my gastrointestinal pipeage. I suddenly realized that I had better relieve myself of what was undoubtedly a buildup of noxious fumes before entering the vehicle. So I slowly strolled around the backside of the BMW while I successfully managed a controlled release of gases from my own backside. Believing that I had successfully avoided a disastrously embarrassing situation, I opened the door, sat in the driver's seat, closed the door behind me, and gave my date a look of confident suavity. To which she replied, "So, it followed you into the car." Apparently there was a residual odor that lingered beyond my recognition.

And so it is with our sin. Whether we are cognizant of it or not, the impact of our sin has a residual effect on our relationship with God. The impact lingers even though we may refuse to acknowledge it. To live in denial of our sin, to expect that our relationship with God continues unaffected, is to deny God's holiness. Acting as if nothing is wrong displays a blatantly unrepentant heart. How can we expect to enjoy an intimate relationship with

God when we are living in defiant disobedience to his precepts? How can we be sincere in our love for a holy God when we have absolutely no regard for his holiness?

Tattoos Are Not a Sin, but They Remind Me of Mine

My cavalier attitude toward God's holiness was revealed to me in a stark and abrupt manner a few years ago. It was the summer after my son graduated from high school, and I was on a cross-country trip with my writing partner. Before I departed, my son and I had an intense discussion about tattoos. He wanted one, and I said no. I told him I didn't have any objection to tattoos, but less-enlightened members of my generation might judge his character by outward appearances. I didn't want his prospects for employment after college graduation to be deterred by depictions on his epidermis that narrow-minded prospective employers wouldn't appreciate. The final words before my departure made clear that he would have no tattoos as long as I was the financial source of his sustenance.

Imagine my fury while traveling somewhere between Chicago and Seattle when my wife called and told me that my punk kid had gotten a tattoo. How dare he? How could he disrespect me so flagrantly? After all I had done for him and sacrificed for his benefit, how could he so easily defy me? I was going to deal harshly with him, so I planned to fly home to Fresno as soon as I reached Seattle. The list of penalties I would impose on him started with cutting off his tuition and got worse from there. The longer I drove, the more trouble he was in.

Then a weird thing happened. Unfortunately, I have no witness to the event that I'm about to describe because my writing partner was asleep in the shotgun seat of the car. But maybe this is the way God wanted it because this was just between him and me. I was driving in silence because radio reception was nonexistent as we drove across Montana. But out of the silence came an audible voice that distinctly said: "What about your tattoos?"

My non-Pentecostal proclivities allowed me to dismiss the voice the first time, but a few moments later it returned. "What about your tattoos?"

Sensing this was a God voice, I replied, "Lord, you know I have no tattoos. My skin is as pure as the new-fallen snow." (I couldn't help myself. I thought a little humor might diffuse the uncomfortable solemnity of the situation.) And then I heard the statement that cut to my heart, a statement I'll always remember (at least I hope I do). God said to me in words that were as penetrating as they were clearly enunciated: "What about the times when you defy me each time you intentionally sin?"

God slew me with that statement. It hurt because it was so true. I recognized defiance in my son's relationship with me, but I was totally oblivious to it in my relationship with God. Many times I had sinned with absolutely no regard to how God felt about it. How dare I do that to him? How could I disrespect him so flagrantly? After all he had done for me and his Son's sacrificial death for my benefit, how could I so easily defy him?

My son escaped much of the punishment I had planned for him. I gladly extended grace and forgiveness to him in acknowledgment of the much greater forgiveness and grace that God had bestowed on me. Both my son and I learned lessons from his tattoo, but my learning curve was greater than his.[12] I had been worshipping a God of my own design—one who wasn't bothered very much by sin. My god was fine with that. The God who is was not.

My son's childish defiance was easy for me to see, but I had been blind to my spiritual defiance of my heavenly Father. I had become insensitive to how much my sin offended and disappointed God because I had conveniently overlooked God's attributes of holiness and righteousness. I had made him into a god I wanted rather than revering him as the God he is. As a result, I had grown comfortable with my sin, and by tolerating sin in my life, I had no chance of experiencing the abundant life that Christ promised I could have.

We are to love God with all of our heart, soul, and strength. But we'll be wasting our time if we're directing that love to a fake god that we formulated according to our own selfish preferences. The real God exists, and part of our wholehearted love requires that we discover and worship him in all his fullness—as he is, not as we prefer him to be. When we remove our misconceptions about him, we will be much more likely to love him because of who he is.

Getting a Glimpse of God

ABANDONING YOUR RELIGION FOR A RELATIONSHIP

Sometimes seeing God is difficult because he gets lost in all of the trappings and extraneous details that we associate with Christianity. We lose sight of him because we're too concerned with doing Christianity correctly. We're too busy looking at ourselves—examining what we're doing and how we're doing it. It's hard to see God when we're preoccupied with looking at ourselves.

Many of us Christians have reduced our faith to a religion (yes, I am complicit). Christianity has been misconstrued—by its own adherents—to be a checklist of things to do and things to refrain from. You get points for checking good things off the list, and you get demerits for doing the bad things on the list. You become a better Christian by following the list religiously, and our gospel message is all about the list instead of our Savior.

Christ-centered believers appropriately recoil at such notions.

But we make a mistake if we reject the teachings of the Old Testament on the erroneous notion that the Ten Commandments are the origin of "checklist Christianity." Moses knew a thing or two (or ten) about the inscriptions on those stone tablets, and he certainly didn't consider them to be a checklist of behavior that qualifies one to be worthy of God's favor. Just the opposite. The Ten Commandments describe a person who is engaged in a love relationship with God.

Moses enumerated the Ten Commandments in one of his farewell addresses to the Israelites (Deuteronomy 5). Several verses later (Deuteronomy 6:5), he summarized the Ten Commandments by entreating the Israelites to simply love God with all their heart, soul, and strength. Instead of saying that the Big Ten are a checklist of required behavior, he presented them as a lifestyle that will naturally follow if one is wholeheartedly in love with God. When viewed from this perspective, the Ten Commandments are more about a relationship than they are about rules to be religiously followed.

Jesus explained the same view of the Ten Commandments when a Pharisee tried to stump him with what seemed to be a theological brainteaser. Of course, it was only a complex theological question for those who viewed the Ten Commandments as rules rather than the lifestyle reflection of a relationship:

> One of [the Pharisees], an expert in religious law, tried to trap [Jesus] with this question: "Teacher, which is the most important commandment in the law of Moses?"
> Jesus replied, "'You must love the LORD your God with all your heart, all your soul, and all your mind.' This is the first and greatest commandment."[13]

Jesus referred to Moses' statement in Deuteronomy. And in so doing, he confirmed that God is more interested in a relationship than a religion of rules and regulations.

I'm the first to admit that I like checklists, especially religious ones. They allow me to conform on the outside without having to be transformed on the inside. (Maybe that is why God abhors them.) And my self-esteem is stroked if I think God loves me better and more than he loves those who don't have as many points as I have accumulated. And sometimes I even get to the outrageous place of suspecting that God is happy to have me on his team because I am such a high achiever: Is it any wonder that he saved someone like me, who has racked up so many points on the checklist?

But then I come crashing back to reality when I realize that God rescued the Israelites from slavery in Egypt *before* he gave them the Ten Commandments. He didn't save them because they were good and followed the checklists. He saved them because *he* is good. God gave them the Ten Commandments in the post-rescue shelter and safety of Mt. Sinai to remind them what a life looks like when it has been dedicated to him. Only *after* he had already extended grace to them did he give them ten descriptive profiles for their appropriate response.

My affinity for checklists is totally misplaced. I like them because I think they make me look good. But I should be using them as a benchmark to see if I'm properly responding to God's goodness. I'm inappropriately using them to bolster my religion, but God wants me to use them as an indicator of the quality of my relationship with him. The apostle Paul says this is the appropriate way to worship God:

> And so, dear brothers and sisters, I plead with you to give your bodies to God because of all he has done for you. Let them be a living and holy sacrifice—the kind he will find acceptable. This is truly the way to worship him.[14]

Paul is saying that our lifestyle and attitudes shouldn't be governed by rules, but should be the outgrowth of our relationship with Christ. When we consider all that God has done for us, shouldn't we desire to live in a manner that pleases him?

◦—

Moses, Jesus, and Paul all agree. We should dump all notions that we relate to God by means of a religion. We should forget the rules and abandon the checklists. They aren't necessary if we are serious about developing a wholehearted, loving relationship with God. If you are only involved in a religion, you won't see God; you've got to be in a relationship with him for that to happen.

...Because I
Don't Want to
Annoy Him with
My Prayers

od made it easy for us to communicate with him. Even science says so. Dr. Andrew B. Newberg is an assistant professor at the University of Pennsylvania with appointments in three departments: Radiology, Psychiatry, and Religious Studies. Seems like a strange mix for an MD, but not when you realize that his research examines how the brain functions when it is engaged in prayer and other religious experiences. Through the use of functional brain imaging, Dr. Newberg has been able to prove that a particular part of the brain is used in prayer. His professional medical opinion is that our brains have been calibrated and hardwired for prayer.[1]

As is usually the case, God is way ahead of science on this one. Thousands of years before Dr. Newberg started probing brain tissue with electrodes, God declared that he programmed us for spiritual sensitivity and "planted eternity in the human heart."[2] We have been specifically designed and crafted by God in a way that allows us to have personal conversations with him. So if a breakdown occurs in our communication with God, it's probably not due to a lack of interest on his part. That leaves the person at the other end of the conversation as the one who needs to work on his or her spiritual communication skills.

$\backsim$

No one likes to say it publicly because it doesn't sound very Christian, but in moments of brutal honesty you might hear someone admit that prayer doesn't seem to be as great as people say it is. God has gone to a lot of trouble to design us for communication with him, so you might think that prayer ought to be a natural and instinctive part of our Christian lives. More than that, it ought to be pretty exciting—after all, you're conversing directly with the Almighty. So why do many of us have prayer lives that are boring, dull, and routine?

Can you commiserate with me on this? If not, you might be the one out of a hundred Christians who has a vibrant conversation going on with God. For the rest of us, our prayers have more to do with our traditions and rituals than our excitement about talking with God.

In the interest of full disclosure, allow me to admit that my statistic that 99 percent of Christians stink at praying is based on no quantitative analysis. But I have heard a lot of Christians pray, and I know a feeble prayer when I hear one (because I've uttered a lot of them myself). Many of our prayers are jabbered out of habit and with absolutely no expectation that the prayer will actually accomplish anything. Let's face it. Most of us pray often, but we do it halfheartedly, and we forget the whole point of it. We're usually on autopilot when we pray, and we lose sight of prayer's true purpose. We say a prayer so we can eat a meal, or we say a prayer before we go to sleep. Sad to say, most of our prayers are passionless (with the exception of the prayer that we scream out as our car slides over a cliff).

Why Should I Tell God What He Already Knows?

Just knowing about God doesn't mean we'll automatically know how to pray. Sure, new Christians face a learning curve, but as we mature in our faith, we also need to grow in our spiritual fluency. Otherwise, a stunted prayer life can sabotage our relationship with Christ.

If we're too impressed with ourselves for knowing a few basics about God, we can fool ourselves into thinking that prayer isn't important or even necessary. Take a look at some of the essential theology that can lead to this erroneous conclusion:

- God is sovereign—all things are under his control.
- God is omnipotent—he has the power to do everything.
- God is omniscient—he knows everything.
- God is loving—he wants what is best for us.
- God is the Lord—we need to be submissive to his will.

When all of this theology is put together, we might correctly conclude that God is in charge of the universe (sovereignty), and he can do whatever he wants (omnipotence). He wants what is best for us (love), and he knows better than we do what that might be (omniscience).

So far, so good. But the next seemingly logical step is where our thinking becomes flawed: We deduce that we shouldn't presume to tell the Creator of the universe what we want. We might ask for the wrong thing or for the right thing at the wrong time. Nope, if we want to play it safe and respect God for who he is, we ought to shut up and take whatever God brings our way (let him be Lord).

Some of us go through this line of thinking in an analytical manner; others of us simply assume it's true. Either way, we conclude that we don't need to bother with praying because God already knows our thoughts and desires.[3] Furthermore, what we wanted might be bad for us, or it might not be as good as what God has in mind. We want his will for our lives anyway, so we are better off to let him handle the entire deal and not waste our time with our possibly inappropriate requests. Sure, we keep praying to God to offer our praise and confession, but for the intimate longings of our heart, we defer to whatever God has in mind without wasting both his time and ours with prayers that seem superfluous. This seems to be our best way to be sure that we experience God's will for our lives, and it has the added benefit of being time efficient.

We've deluded ourselves into thinking we're being spiritual by allowing God to deal directly with our concerns instead of inserting ourselves into the process. So we simply don't bother him with what we consider to be redundant prayers about our health, career, family, goals, and finances. We stop praying about the things that are most important to us.

No wonder the remnants of our prayer life (praise and confession) become increasingly less effective and enjoyable, and we become less inclined to pray at all. After a while, our entire prayer life seems rather useless, so we wonder why we are doing it at all, even the praise and confession part.

Two Parables About Pestering Prayers

When all else fails, go to the Bible. That's what I did in an attempt to extract myself from the pathetic prayer pit I had dug myself into. I reread two parables that Jesus used to teach us what prayer is like. A cursory reading of these parables seemed to confirm my theology about not pestering God with my requests. Or so I thought. Here's the first one:

> Suppose you went to a friend's house at midnight, wanting to borrow three loaves of bread. You say to him, "A friend of mine has just arrived for a visit, and I have nothing for him to eat." And suppose he calls out from his bedroom, "Don't bother me.

The door is locked for the night, and my family and I are all in bed. I can't help you." But I tell you this—though he won't do it for friendship's sake, if you keep knocking long enough, he will get up and give you whatever you need because of your shameless persistence.[4]

And here's the second one:

There was a judge in a certain city...who neither feared God nor cared about people. A widow of that city came to him repeatedly, saying, "Give me justice in this dispute with my enemy." The judge ignored her for a while, but finally he said to himself, "I don't fear God or care about people, but this woman is driving me crazy. I'm going to see that she gets justice, because she is wearing me out with her constant requests!"[5]

In a feeble attempt to apply these parables to my own situation, I put myself into the stories. The assignment of roles seemed obvious. In the first parable, I was the pesky host with unexpected company in the middle of the night, and God was the harassed neighbor who couldn't get to sleep because I kept pounding on his door. In the second parable, I was the widow who incessantly annoyed the judge (God) until he complied with my request out of exasperation with me.

My exegesis of these Bible passages seemed to support my theory that God doesn't want to be bothered with certain prayer requests. In both parables, I (the host or the widow) appeared to be irritating and infuriating God (the neighbor or the judge). I've read enough of the Old Testament to know that irritating and infuriating God is not wise. If you doubt my logic, go back and read the parables. The neighbor doesn't seem to be very pleased with the host, and the judge certainly has no fondness for the widow (the "driving me crazy" reference is a clue). So the Bible supported my practice of prayer request restraint. Or so I thought.

As it turns out, my exegetical analysis was way off. Come to find out, Jesus never intended for each individual element in a parable to correspond to a specific item outside the story. We should not interpret parables by making direct comparisons, but that's what I did. With my preconceived theology about God and prayer, I was using these stories to turn a prayer request into something God didn't want to hear. I didn't want to pester God and push him to the point of exasperation. I didn't want to annoy God so much that he eventually said, "That guy is driving me crazy. I'm going to see that he gets what he wants because he is wearing me out with his constant requests." I loved God too much to do that to him.

My reasoning was based on a fatal flaw. I had failed to realize that these parables were simply stories intended to illustrate a single point—a point that I had missed in its entirety. I was somehow oblivious to the clear lesson: God wants us to come to him with our requests, and he is eager to grant them. But what about the neighbor and the judge? Well, I had mistakenly attributed the characteristics and responses of the neighbor and judge to God. But God *isn't* like the cranky neighbor, because God cares for me. (He allowed his only Son to be crucified for my benefit, so he certainly wouldn't mind getting up in the middle of the night to rustle up some crackers and cheese for me.) And God *isn't* the judge—which I should have known from the parable's indication that the judge was dishonest and heartless.

I had missed the contrast of these parables: If a cranky neighbor complies, and if the callous judge relents, then how much more will my loving and gracious heavenly Father be inclined to respond to requests from his children, whom he loves? Wow. How could I have missed these obvious interpretations?

But that's not all. There's more. Besides the striking contrast of God's openness to the petitions from his people, both of these parables actually affirm and endorse the relentless and persistent efforts of the petitioner. I had missed the predicate to both of these parables, so I had missed a key component of the parables themselves.

Immediately after telling the parable of the host and the neighbor, Jesus said, "And so I tell you, keep on asking, and you will receive what you ask for. Keep on seeking, and you will find. Keep on knocking, and the door will be opened to you."[6] And immediately preceding the parable of the widow and the judge, Luke tells us the reason why Christ told the parable in the first place: "One day Jesus told his disciples a story to show that they should always pray and never give up."[7]

For years I had this prayer thing backward. In my arrogance and pride, I had been interpreting biblical principles about prayer to fit my own twisted theology. In so doing, I was insulting God and depriving myself of intimate (and productive) conversation with him.

It won't be difficult for you to realize why I felt chided and convicted when I came across this quote in my devotional reading one morning:

> It is an insult to sink before God and say, "Your will be done" when there has been no intercession. That is the prayer of impertinent unbelief—there is no use in praying, "God does whatever He chooses." The saying of "Your will be done" is born of the most intimate relationship to God whereby I talk to Him freely. Repetition in intercessory importunity is not bargaining, but the joyous insistence of prayer.[8]

That sentiment is precisely the message of these two parables. Those of us who have been living in a melancholic prayer coma have somehow managed to overlook the crucial theology these parables give us. We're not pestering God when we pray to him. He is eager to hear our requests (even though he knows what we'll be saying before the words come out of our mouths). And he doesn't consent to our requests begrudgingly; rather, he will generously give us even more than we ask for. And that's the point: We have to actually ask.

Passionate Prayer

Applying the principles of Scripture to your life is easier if you understand them correctly in the first place. And an enlightened understanding of the prayer parables will inevitably open our eyes to the biblical concept of passionate prayer. It has been there all along, but many of us have somehow missed it. As the New Testament writer James says, "The earnest prayer of a righteous person has great power and produces wonderful results."[9]

I'm no Bible scholar (as proven by my original hatchet job on the prayer parables), but this seems to be a fairly straightforward promise. It entails three elements. First, you start with an earnest prayer. The word "earnest" seems a little limp if you're thinking it merely means "sincere." But the more common definition of "earnest" fits the context: an attitude characterized by an intense and serious state of mind. I translate that as *passionate*. In other words, we're talking about a prayer that is enthusiastic and impassioned. Nothing routine or mundane about it. This kind of prayer is extreme.

The next element requires that a righteous person prays the prayer. "Righteous" doesn't mean the person is wholly holy, but that he or she is on good terms with God, living according to his precepts, and praying in submission to his overriding will. When you put those two elements together—the passionate prayer from a righteous person—you get the third element of the promise: great and wonderful results.

Perhaps you've noticed that the promise of James 5:16 doesn't go so far as to say that we'll get what we pray for. It simply says that the passionate prayer of a righteous person will produce great and wonderful results. But "great and wonderful" is certainly not a consolation prize. God is the one who determines what is great and wonderful, so we have a divine guarantee that God's response will be better than what we would have gotten if he had granted our prayer exactly as we recited it.

The bottom line of James 5:16 is simply this: The passionate prayer of a righteous person works. And isn't that what you and I have been looking for all along? We just want prayer that *works*.

The two prerequisites for prayer that works—passion and righteousness—don't come easy. They require more than saying "Pleeeeeeze" (notice the passionate emphasis) after being on your best behavior for the preceding 24 hours (to fulfill the qualification of righteousness). The exemplar for us to follow in this regard is none other than Christ when he was praying in the garden at the Mount of Olives shortly before he was arrested.[10] Because this was Jesus, we know he satisfied the "righteous" criterion for prayer that works. He had that whole sinless thing going for him that we can never achieve, but that doesn't mean we're perennially disqualified from the "righteous" component of James 5:16. The righteousness of Christ in the garden of Gethsemane on that evening was not his sinlessness; it was his willingness to accept God's plan even if that plan contravened Christ's specific prayer request. Christ was pleading with his heavenly Father for an alternative route for humanity's salvation—something less drastic than crucifixion. But his prayer was couched in submission to God's ultimate will: "Please take this cup of suffering away from me. Yet I want your will to be done, not mine."[11]

We know how the story ended, so we know that God didn't spare Christ from that cup of suffering. But true to the promise of James, Christ's prayer for God's ultimate will produced great and wonderful results by providing us with a sacrifice for our sins that makes our eternal salvation and relationship with God possible.

As for the passion of Christ's prayer, the Bible gives us graphic descriptions:

- "He took Peter, James, and John with him, and he became deeply troubled and distressed. He told them, 'My soul is crushed with grief to the point of death.'"[12]
- "He prayed more fervently, and he was in such agony

of spirit that his sweat fell to the ground like great drops of blood."[13]

We are not required to sweat blood in order to pray passionately. After all, Jesus was facing the prospect of taking on himself the sin of the world and the accompanying agony and torture of crucifixion. We can never come close to that kind of passion. But we need more intensity than we exhibit when we cavalierly mumble a prayer in the car (*God, please help the stock market to go up today because my 401[k] account sucks*). And we need more fervor than we use to recite a ritualistic monthly mantra (*Lord, help me make wise choices at my spa appointment today*).

A passionate prayer is authentic because it is heartfelt; it includes an aspect of intimacy between us and God. And a passionate prayer is intense; we become relentless in bringing our request before God because it is so important to us.

Putting God to Work

I've come a long way from my prior theology of not wanting to pester God with my prayers. Now I am pestering (make that *entreating*) him all of the time. More than that, I'm expecting that my prayers will actually put him to work. Previously, I was expecting to do the work myself to bring about what I was praying for. Now I've come to realize that according to James, when I pray, I put God to work.

Those previous prayers of mine were mediocre and fainthearted. My faith in God's ability wasn't weak; I positively knew he was able to deliver what I had been praying for. But my prayers were pathetic because my theology was wrong. I thought God would respond to my prayer only if he wanted to. To my surprise, the Bible says that God is withholding his intervention in my life in response to my prayers until I start praying passionately. But once I begin praying with intensity, then (and only then) God will respond.

At the end of the parable about the host and his neighbor, Jesus explained that God is actually eager to bless his children:

> Everyone who asks, receives. Everyone who seeks, finds. And to everyone who knocks, the door will be opened.
>
> You fathers—if your children ask for a fish, do you give them a snake instead? Or, if they ask for an egg, do you give them a scorpion? Of course not! So if you sinful people know how to give good gifts to your children, how much more will your heavenly Father give the Holy Spirit to those who ask him.[14]

Here again, I struggle a bit with the theology of it all, but I've learned to read the Bible for what it says and not merely to support my self-conceived notion of how God operates. Whether I'm comfortable with the notion or not, Scripture tells me that my passionate prayers for receiving, finding, and opening will be answered when (and only when) I commence and continue with the asking, the seeking, and the knocking.

"You don't have what you want because you don't ask God for it."[15] Prayer involves asking. And if we aren't asking, we aren't praying.

All those years when I was living a bland and prosaic Christian life, I could have had a dynamic and vibrant one. I thought I was being polite by waiting for God to kick things into gear because I didn't want to presume on his timing. In actuality, he was the one who was patiently waiting for me to abandon my view of how he operates and to get on board with his divine design. I could have received, but I didn't ask. And God responds to the asking.

◦—

When we pray the way God intends, we'll be face-to-face with him in conversation. In that position, you'll have absolutely no problem in seeing God. You can't miss him. He's the one who is hanging on your every word.

BEING YOURSELF WHEN YOU PRAY

Being cordial to someone is different from feeling close to them. We can be cordial to strangers or people with whom we are only slightly acquainted. It isn't difficult; we just need to be polite and pleasant with them. But we remain guarded and won't tell them too much about our personal lives. We're leery of how they might use or misuse personal information. Close friends, however, get a different treatment. Around them, we can relax because we trust them. They get the privilege, and sometimes the burden, of knowing what is actually going on in our lives.

God doesn't want to be your acquaintance. He prefers and deserves the privileged status reserved for a closest friend. When we think of him that way, we'll be more at ease in his presence.

~

The concept of prayer can be intimidating: human beings conversing with Almighty God! But when we look at it from the perspective that we're God's children, we see that conversing with him should be as natural as children talking to their father. You might not be a father, but there is a high probability that you've been a child. Your relationship with your biological father might have made communication difficult at various times in your life, but that doesn't have to be the case with your heavenly Father.

First and foremost, God wants us to approach him without pretense. He wants us to be open, honest, and transparent. This is difficult for many of us to do; we tend to lack authenticity in our prayers because we are too intent on impressing

God (or those who might be listening to our prayers). We're more concerned about how we are being judged by the hearers (God or the other members of our prayer circle) than we are about the subject of our prayers. Thus our prayers become performances.

We might notice some telltale signs when this is happening. For instance, do you customarily speak in an urban vernacular but shift into the King's English when you pray? I don't want to seem sacrilegious by using a real prayer, so I'll simply employ a ditty that most everyone is familiar with. You might have a "performance prayer" problem if you regularly talk like this...

> You put your left leg in; you put your left leg out.
> You put your left leg in and you shake it all about.
> You do the Hokey Pokey, and you turn yourself around.
> That's what it's all about.

But when you pray, it sounds like this...

> O proud right foot that ventures quick within,
> Then soon upon a backward journey moves.
> Anon, once more the gesture to begin:
> Next command that appendage pedestal to groove.
> Commence thou then the fervid hokey-poke:
> A mad gyration; hips in wanton swirl.
> To spin! A wide release from heaven's yoke.
> Blessed dervish! Surely canst thou go, girl.
> The hoke, the poke—banish not thy doubt.
> Verily, I say, 'Tis what it's all about.[16]

You get the idea. Whether for God's benefit or to impress others, pretense in our prayer life will prevent us from talking honestly with God.

Coming to God as yourself also involves a degree of self-assessment. As we approach God in prayer, we need to humble ourselves, not thinking too highly of ourselves. But neither should we consider ourselves to be so wretched that God doesn't extend his love to us. We need to balance our humility with our confidence that God's love makes us worthy in his eyes. Christ's parable explains the balance, identifying one guy who lacked any sort of balance and one who achieved it:

> Two men went to the Temple to pray. One was a Pharisee, and the other was a despised tax collector. The Pharisee stood by himself and prayed this prayer: "I thank you, God, that I am not a sinner like everyone else. For I don't cheat, I don't sin, and I don't commit adultery. I'm certainly not like that tax collector! I fast twice a week, and I give you a tenth of my income."
>
> But the tax collector stood at a distance and dared not even lift his eyes to heaven as he prayed. Instead, he beat his chest in sorrow, saying, "God, be merciful to me, for I am a sinner." I tell you, this sinner, not the Pharisee, returned home justified before God. For those who exalt themselves will be humbled, and those who humble themselves will be exalted.[17]

God wants us to get past the charade and get to a place of honesty. Only then will we be in a position where he can alleviate our worries in the prayer process. He wants us in a worry-free place—relinquishing our cares and concerns to him. His process is prayer, and the place is called peace.

> Don't worry about anything; instead, pray about everything. Tell God what you need, and thank him for all he has done. Then you will experience God's peace, which exceeds anything we can understand. His peace will guard your hearts and minds as you live in Christ Jesus.[18]

To obtain the peace that God promises, we need to have legitimate conversations with him. We can't go for efficiency or brevity. "Dear God, please solve all my problems; you know what they are; take care of them and snap to it!" That kind of prayer might work under emergency circumstances, but it isn't what the psalmist had in mind when he encouraged us to "wait patiently for the LORD."[19] We are told to pray about everything, but not all together in one single breath.

Think of a new mother who is leaving her infant child with a babysitter for the very first time. The mother doesn't say, "Take care of my kid and call me if you need me." Maternal instincts don't allow that kind of generality. Instead, the mother will give the sitter very detailed and specific instructions for every eventuality concerning food, milk, diapers, blankie, and binkie. The emergency phone call list will include the mother's cell phone, the phone numbers for every place she'll stop, and maybe even the places she'll be driving by en route. The sitter will end up knowing the baby's blood type, birthday, Social Security number, and grandmothers' maiden names. In other words, the sitter will have total familiarity with every aspect of the child, who is so important to that mother.

That same kind of specificity is what God wants to hear from us. He desires that we speak with him, plainly and patiently, about every single one of our concerns. The articulation of our individual anxieties is not for his benefit; it is for ours. We need to release that angst to him in the context of sensing his care and his control. But honesty and candor are required so we can realize the full extent of his peace.

If we attempt to stay cloaked in privacy or pretend to be someone other than who we really are, God is not fooled. Our privacy creates no mystery for him, and our pretending is transparent. We're only fooling ourselves to think that God can't see through the charade.

～

The prayers of a disingenuous person are nothing more than hollow, ineffectual words. But God will respond when we pray intensely and specifically in humility without affectation or pride. God may be invisible while we speak our prayers, but we'll see him clearly in the circumstances that his responses produce.

...Because the
Abundant Life
Seems like
a Myth

The apostle Peter shines as a Christian superstar in a few biblical passages. I don't relate to him very well on these occasions. Take this one, for example:

> When Jesus came to the region of Caesarea Philippi, he asked his disciples, "Who do people say that the Son of Man is?"
>
> "Well," they replied, "some say John the Baptist, some say Elijah, and others say Jeremiah or one of the other prophets."
>
> Then he asked them, "But who do you say I am?"
>
> Simon Peter answered, "You are the Messiah, the Son of the living God."
>
> Jesus replied, "You are blessed, Simon son of John, because my Father in heaven has revealed this to you. You did not learn this from any human being. Now I say to you that you are Peter (which means "rock"), and upon this rock I will build my church, and all the powers of hell will not conquer it. And I will give you the keys of the Kingdom of Heaven. Whatever you forbid on

earth will be forbidden in heaven, and whatever you permit on earth will be permitted in heaven."[1]

After Peter received those accolades from Christ, can't you just picture him walking around and strutting his spiritual stuff? But you don't have to wait too long for Peter to fall off his pedestal and goof up his Christianity. Those are the times when I think that he and I could be buds. Like the time, only two verses after the passage above, when Jesus chastises him for being unspiritual:

> From then on Jesus began to tell his disciples plainly that it was necessary for him to go to Jerusalem, and that he would suffer many terrible things at the hands of the elders, the leading priests, and the teachers of religious law. He would be killed, but on the third day he would be raised from the dead.
> But Peter took him aside and began to reprimand him for saying such things. "Heaven forbid, Lord," he said. "This will never happen to you!"
> Jesus turned to Peter and said, "Get away from me, Satan! You are a dangerous trap to me. You are seeing things merely from a human point of view, not from God's."[2]

What a dunce! Even I know that reprimanding Jesus Christ is not wise. And if Jesus calls you "Satan," well, that can't be good. But to be honest with myself, I have to admit that I'm no better than Peter in this episode, for I too look at God's paradigm from a human point of view.

⌒

I can't speak for the rest of the world, but those of us in the United States seem to spend a lot of time contemplating life rather than living it. For many of us, our primary goal in life is to find meaning and purpose in it. A casual stroll through a bookstore will support this supposition. For example, Bob Buford's best-selling book *Halftime* encourages old duffers (my term, not his, although he seems to be writing to the over-50 crowd) to look for significance in their second half of life because they settled for success in the first half.

This obsession with meaning and purpose isn't limited to those who have lived a prolonged but empty life. It's also common among those whose life journey hasn't been long enough to qualify as a short walk. The "quarterlife crisis" books are replete with quotes from twentysomethings bemoaning the difficulty of finding passion and meaning in world around them.[3] Bottom line: Getting started in life is difficult without knowing your purpose in advance. (This rationale is not persuasive with most parents who have just depleted their 401[k] to pay for their child's college education. But it's worth a try if you're negotiating a parental subsidy for that post-graduation, yearlong backpack trip across Europe or free room and board in your parents' home while you try to find yourself.)

This search is very introspective. After all, what constitutes meaning, purpose, and passion will be different for each one of us. At the epicenter is the emphasis on identity, self-worth, and self-esteem. So it is an individual thing.

Not surprisingly, this perspective has invaded our collective psyche. We've been raised in a culture steeped in existentialism. Even people who believe in God and reject the existential notion that the universe lacks meaning or purpose are likely to adhere to the concomitant principle that individual meaning is an individual quest. Our intellectual assent to such beliefs is evident in our behavior: We continually juggle and manipulate the various components in our lives (such as work, family, recreation, public service, and faith) to find the mix that gives us the most satisfaction. We go to the smorgasbord of life and fill up on the portions we want, skipping those that don't seem appetizing to us. (Personally, I'm not fond of political activism, so you won't find much of that on my plate. But I'm glad that others find it nourishing in their lives. They can have my portion.)

Christians throw God, church, and the Bible into the mix. Those are certainly essential components in our lives. But we still retain the freedom—nay, the perceived inalienable right—to decide on the allocations. Most of us want God to have a place in our lives, but we want to determine the size and priority of the God component. We wouldn't want too much of a God thing. We don't want it to intrude on other aspects of our lives from which we might derive secular meaning, purpose, and pleasure. Thus, even with God in our lives, we still consider that we are our own authoritative voice.

In this process, we are like Peter, viewing spiritual matters "merely from a human point of view."

But the self-centeredness of existentialism is just the opposite of God's plan. He wants and deserves to be the sole source of meaning and purpose in our lives. God desires to allocate and moderate the components of our lives so that our passion and purpose are realized in him as the Holy Spirit works in and through us.

The Promise and the Paradox

Many of us Christians see nothing wrong with being the captain of our own ship, charting a course in search of meaning and purpose. We know for certain that a life of such substance exists because Christ himself promised it to us.

> Yes, I am the gate. Those who come in through me will be saved. They will come and go freely and will find good pastures. The thief's purpose is to steal and kill and destroy. My purpose is to give them a rich and satisfying life.[4]

For purposes of clarification, a "rich and satisfying life" does not imply riches (despite how proponents of the prosperity gospel might interpret this verse). Christ did not come to earth to make us financially wealthy. He wasn't really worried about our comfort and safety. Just ask any of the first-century Christians. Oh, wait— you can't ask them because they are dead, having been tortured to death in the Roman Coliseum because of their allegiance to

Christ. But I guess that proves my point. Christ was all about turning from your selfish ways, taking up your cross, and following him.[5] (That whole "take up your cross" and crucifixion metaphor has got to throw a kink in the prosperity gospel.)

Christ's promise of a rich and satisfying life must be understood in its complete spiritual context. Regardless of our financial circumstances, Christ promised us a life that is "abundant," "full," "real and eternal—more and better than we ever dreamed of," and "enjoyable and overflowing."[6]

Thus, our life, regardless of how difficult our circumstances, can be filled with meaning, purpose, and passion. We don't have to wait until the kingdom comes in its fullness. We can have that kind of life right here, right now. No wonder those first-century Christians were willing to die for this kind of life. A life void of such meaning and purpose hardly seems worth living.

This brings us to the paradox of the Christian life. Christ promised us a life of passion and completeness, but many of us don't seem to have found it even though we're searching diligently for it. This can't be Christ's fault. He doesn't seem like a cruel prankster who would hide from us what he wants us to have. Certainly he is not reneging on his promise. So in good faith, relying on his promise, we continue the search for a life of purpose and passion. And until we find it, our Christianity isn't working too well for many of us. It is not necessarily a struggle, but it isn't very thrilling either. It is just kind of bland.

When confronted with this paradox (reading the John 10:10 promise of a full life and yet feeling empty and lifeless inside), we have three choices:

Quit the Christian Life

Some have chosen this option. The rest of us might be tempted, but we realize that quitting the Christian life doesn't solve the problem. First, we have no promising alternatives. Second, we'll always wonder if we simply quit too soon to give Christianity a fair shot. Maybe the promised life of passion would have kicked in if we stayed with Christianity a little longer. As G.K. Chesterton said, "Christianity has not been tried and found wanting; it has been found difficult and not tried." That is where many of the quitters got off track. It's not that Christianity is flawed; rather, it wasn't tried the way God designed it.

Keep Failing at the Christian Life

Some may think that even a mediocre Christian life is better than a life outside the Christian community. After all, most Christians are pleasant people (at least when they are in church). Many churches are like social country clubs: The membership gathers at frequent intervals, everyone dresses nicely, you meet in a beautiful facility, membership provides you with manufactured friendships that you might not be able to forge on your own, and you get served food and beverage from time to time (occasionally at church social events, or at least when the communion elements are distributed). So even if you can't attain the abundant life of John 10:10, you at least have an option of filling your life with religious activities.

Fake the Christian Life

This is where Christianity blends with those positive mental attitude seminars (and a lot of multilevel marketing schemes). Their mantra is "Fake it till you make it." They say you'll never change your circumstances for the better if you're stuck with "stinkin' thinkin'." So even though your track record is miserable, they want you to project an image of success. Fool others, and soon you'll fool yourself, and eventually you'll become the successful person you've been pretending to be. Sound familiar? Know any Christians who have been playing this same game? They are still failing at the Christian life, but they pretend otherwise.

For those of us who are sincere in our search for a life of meaning and purpose, none of these choices is satisfactory. Each one leaves us with a life that is less than what we want and far less than what Christ promises to us. So we continue our search, anxious to find meaning and purpose in our faith, but coming up less than satisfied. Something deep inside haunts us. But something tells us that the abundant life shouldn't be so difficult to attain. Could it be that we ourselves are the problem? Certainly not us, because we're genuine, candid, and diligent in our search for passion and purpose. But maybe the problem is that we're more sincere in our *search* than we are in our *faith*.

T-ball Christianity

I'm about to embark on an analogy to illustrate an answer to the paradox of the abundant life (why many of us are frantically searching for what God so plainly promised to us), but this analogy will be lost on you unless you have attended a T-ball game. Being a participant in a T-ball game as a kid doesn't count; you must have experienced the activity from the perspective of an outside, objective observer.

I had absolutely no exposure to T-ball until my wife enrolled our five-year-old son on a team. At first, I was horrified because it seemed as if someone had taken my beloved sport of baseball and infiltrated the rules with the doctrines of Communism. Think about it. In T-ball, no one keeps score, no one keeps track of outs, everyone gets a turn at bat in every inning, and the game ends with no loser because both teams are winners. That's athletic socialism: designing the game around the abilities of the weakest player on the team and encouraging everyone to aspire to that level. I cringed at this philosophy, but it worked out well for my son. Rather than being ridiculed by the others, his combined low level of ability and marginal interest made him the one who set the standard of performance for our T-ball league. He was the lowest common denominator—a distinction any father would be proud of.

I can't put all the blame on my son because he was born into a gene pool that was deficient in athleticism. So his lack of physical ability and coordination was not his fault. But he amplified the hilarity of his on-field bloopers by his complete indifference to the game. When his team was on the field, my son knew to assume his solitary post in far right field. (Apparently even when you aren't keeping score, the coach wants his weakest glove in right field.) Outfielders get lonely in T-ball because no ball is hit past the pitcher's mound (which is an oxymoron because T-ball has no pitcher). The other urchin outfielders managed to stay mentally in the game, but not my son. The game bored him, so he turned to his own devices for entertainment. Spectators in the stands were also entertained by his antics in right field as they watched him put his glove on his head and prance around, trying to make monster shapes with his shadow. Sometimes he stayed out there while his team came off the field and took their turn at bat. The coach didn't disturb my son from his prancing; after all, this was T-ball, and no one wanted to jeopardize my son's self-esteem for the sake of following the rules.

By looking at his uniform, you'd never know that my son was a prancer instead of a player. In fact, every uniform on the team looked as if it had been used by a Golden Glove–winning major leaguer. They were stained with grass and dirt even though most of the kids never worked up a sweat or skidded in the grass to field a ball. Sliding into a base wasn't even allowed (again, with the rules intended to bring skills down to the lowest common denominator). I asked my son how his uniform came to look so well-worn. It turns out that on the first day uniforms were issued and worn, all of the kids rolled in the grass and dirt so they would look like real players. I was fascinated. My son didn't know how to play the game—he didn't even like the game—yet he knew how good baseball players looked, and he wanted to emulate them (in appearance only).

And so it is with Christianity. (At long last, the application of the metaphor.) The answer to the paradox of the abundant life is illustrated by my son playing T-ball. Christians are on a team of sorts.

For a long time, I've been in the lineup, but my mind hasn't been in the game. I'm out there prancing in right field, making shadow shapes on the grass. From all outward appearances, people might suspect that I'm an all-star Christian. I wear a uniform that gives that false impression. I have strategically placed grass stains that mislead people to believe that I'm a player when I'm really just a prancer: I attend church regularly, I know and spout Bible verses at appropriate times, I lead a small group, I pray in public. Yep, I look like a player. Only God and I know the pathetic truth that sometimes I can't even hit the spiritual ball off the T.

During the many hours that I've devoted to carefully placing grass stains on my uniform, my spiritual muscles have atrophied. I've been more interested in eating the snack at the end of each game than in improving my spiritual athleticism. The problem is not with the game. The problem is with me. I haven't put my heart, soul, and strength into playing.

Empty Rituals

Let's move on from the T-ball metaphor to a more convicting comparison. When we search the Bible for Christians to emulate, we can't help but be drawn to the commitment and passion of those who were part of the earliest Christian church as reported in Acts. What a group! Their excitement couldn't be contained. They experienced danger, self-sacrifice, and miracles. The persecution by the Roman government and by the Jewish hierarchy did not keep these believers from daily increasing in number. There was something contagious and passionate about the way they lived and the way they loved the Lord and each other.

That's the kind of meaning and purpose we want in our lives. We intuitively sense that if we want the life they had, we need to copy what they did. We read that they prayed a lot, so we pray. They worshipped, so we worship. They fellowshipped, so we hang out with more Christians more often. But going through these religious motions is just more of the same old, same old. Our prayer, worship, and fellowship are manufactured; they don't flow naturally from our love for God. Oh, we love him, but we seem to be less than fully devoted to him. Our lives are not wrapped with him at the center. We go through the motions because we read that these were the things that passionate Christians did. But they did these things in response to the zeal they had for God; we do them as rituals in an attempt to manufacture excitement in our spiritual lives. Their actions were passionate; our imitation of their behavior is meaningless and empty.

If you've ever found yourself in this condition, you know that going through the motions is nothing more than a sad and sorry excuse for the spiritual life God wants us to experience. We can hope that God doesn't realize what is going on, but there is not a chance in heaven that we're fooling him.

> And so the Lord says, "These people say they are mine. They honor me with their lips, but their hearts are far away from me. And their worship of me is nothing but man-made rules learned by rote."[7]

I'm like Samson, Only Not as Buff

I like the Bible for its honesty. More specifically, I like that the Bible doesn't gloss over the spiritual failings of its heroes. More personally, I am grateful to God that the Bible includes some biographies of everyday people who don't set unattainable standards. Both the Old and New Testaments have a large share of spiritual losers; when I read their stories, I still feel bad about my own condition, but at least I know I'll always have something in common with a few folks in the kingdom.

One of the guys I'll be hanging with is Samson. If you see us standing together, you'll know immediately who is who. Our physiques may be different as night and day, but that doesn't mean he and I don't have anything in common. Actually, we do: We suffered the same spiritual ailment.

Samson was a judge in Israel, but he is more famous for his physical (and sexual) exploits.[8] This was during a time when Israel was constantly engaged in battles with its archenemies, the Philistines. As a leader, Samson should have been a spiritual example for the Israelites. Instead, he was the poster boy for *Judges Gone Wild*.

Samson had a history of taunting the Philistines. The Bible recounts several episodes when he unleashed his personal vengeance against them:

- He killed 30 men in retaliation for a prank that the Philistines played on him.

- He caught 300 foxes, tied their tails together in pairs, fastened a torch to each pair, and let the foxes run through the grain fields of the Philistines.

- He killed 1000 Philistines with the jawbone of a donkey.

- In the middle of the night, he pulled up the two posts and the door of the town gate and implanted them on the top of a hill several miles away.[9]

Even though Samson was a buff guy to begin with, the Bible repeatedly reports that these displays of superhuman strength occurred when "the Spirit of the LORD came powerfully upon him."[10] There is a reason for this. As a newborn child, Samson had been dedicated to the Lord in the religious order of the Nazarites, and an angel had prophesied that Samson was chosen by God to rescue Israel from Philistine domination and oppression.[11]

Samson couldn't control his temper, but his downfall came from his failure to control his libido. He fell in love with a Philistine woman, Delilah, who was a covert operative for the Philistine hit squad. She accepted a bribe to learn the secret of Samson's strength so the Philistines could capture him. Basically, they were looking for Samson's kryptonite. The scenario of her deception went like this:

- During a passionate interlude, she asked Samson about his strength. He lied to her and said that he was powerless when tied with seven new bowstrings. So the Philistines tied Samson with seven new bowstrings while he slept in her house. When he awoke, he broke free and busted up a few Philistines.

- Shortly thereafter, Delilah asked again, and Samson said that he couldn't break free if tied with brand new ropes. Again, while he slept, the Philistines tied Samson with new, never-used ropes. Again they woke him, he snapped the ropes and snapped the Philistines.

- Delilah asked a third time. This time Samson responded with a more creative story: "Weave the seven braids of my hair into the fabric of your loom." This also proved to be a fabrication. Samson awoke with his hair in the loom and bashed a few Philistines heads as he escaped.[12]

At this point in the narrative, you begin to realize three things about this odd couple: Delilah was relentless, Samson was big but he was dumb, and Samson must have been a very heavy sleeper. But there is more to the story.

For a *fourth* time, Delilah asked Samson the secret of his strength. In his naïveté, Samson told her that his strength was in his hair. (As a Nazarite dedicated to God, his hair had never been cut.) That night, while he slept, Delilah got out her scissors and razor and went to work. As had happened three times before, Samson awoke. But this time, the now-bald Samson was powerless. The Philistines captured him, gouged out his eyes, and put him in prison, where he pushed a grinding wheel all day.[13]

The secret of Samson's strength was not in his uncut hair, although his lengthy locks had spiritual symbolism and significance. His supernatural power came from God as God chose to bestow it. But Samson was clueless to this fact at the time of his capture: "When he woke up, he thought, 'I will do as before and shake myself free.'

But he didn't realize the LORD had left him."[14] In my humble but correct opinion, that has to be one of the saddest verses in the Bible: Samson didn't realize that the Spirit of the Lord had left him.

The Holy Spirit Is the Missing Component

And here is the point at which Samson and I become so similar. We are like spiritual twin brothers, separated at birth and by about 3200 years. I believe my struggle to find the abundant life that Christ promised was due to the fact that I was slow to realize that I was living outside the penetrating influence of the Holy Spirit.

Without intending to push the Samson analogy too far, you'll remember that when Samson was captured, he was tied up, his eyes were gouged out, and he was put to work grinding grain. In other words, he lost his power, he lost his vision, and life for him was a grind. And that accurately describes how many Christians feel as we stumble around, searching for the abundant life that seems so elusive to us. We have no spiritual power, we have no spiritual vision, and our Christian life is a grind.

We haven't been totally ignorant of the Holy Spirit. We know that the Holy Spirit immediately indwells every believer at the point of salvation and that he stays with us from then forward.[15] But we have gradually become indifferent to his power in our lives. Without availing ourselves of his power, we try to gut through the Christianity gig on our own and in our own strength. We've been depriving ourselves of the essence of what the Holy Spirit offers: divine strength and guidance in our lives.

Here is the crux of the problem: We've been indwelled by the Holy Spirit, but we haven't been filled with the Holy Spirit.[16] Thus, our spiritual lives have lacked the power that the Holy Spirit can provide, they have lacked the vision and guidance that the Holy Spirit can give, and they have lacked the sense of purpose that the Holy Spirit can bring.[17]

This book is not the place for a theological treatise on the Holy

Spirit. There are plenty of sources available for that kind of study. But if you are like me, further study is only part of the answer. We aren't lacking information about the Holy Spirit; we are just living without his input. We've been proud to be searching for spiritual meaning and purpose on our own, ignoring all the while that God was waiting patiently for us to rely on his Holy Spirit to guide us in the search and bring us into the passionate faith we so desperately desired.

⌒

"The Spirit is God's guarantee that he will give us the inheritance he promised."[18]

Christ promised to every believer an inheritance of an abundant life. In our own power, we'll spend a lifetime looking for it but always come up empty-handed. A passionate Christian life will seem like a myth if we depend on ourselves to manufacture it. If we want to attain it, we need to allow the Holy Spirit to be active in our lives. Allowing the Holy Spirit to flourish in our lives will bring us vision, power, and purpose. Our lives will then be energized because God's presence will be so obvious to us. We will see God clearly as never before.

Getting a Glimpse of God

LETTING LOVE BE YOUR MOTIVATION FOR OBEDIENCE

God uses some activities to forge our spiritual lives, such as prayer, Bible study, financial stewardship, and fellowship with other believers in the community of a local church. As Christians, we know the importance of these activities, but at times they seem like monotonous chores. Nonetheless, like good Christian soldiers, we commit ourselves to these spiritual disciplines because we feel obligated. God told us that we need to do them, so we comply even though the burden seems oppressive. As we grow more miserable in the process, God seems farther from us. How ironic: The very things we are doing to draw us closer to God seem to be the cause of our increasing spiritual dissatisfaction.

My son worked as a youth pastor in Seattle for a while. He regularly gave devotional messages to his high school students, but occasionally he was asked to preach the sermon in the "big church." For a series focusing on struggles in the Christian life, the senior pastor asked my son to preach about the tension for single Christians to remain sexually pure. My son consulted with me as he was doing his sermon prep work, but I don't think that any of my insights survived the final edit, and they were left unanalyzed in his computer's trash file. I heard the sermon, and it was good, but all I remember about it is the title: "Sexless in Seattle."

Although my suggestions didn't make the cut, his sermon got me thinking a lot about sexual fidelity. My thought process went something like this: Before I was married, my prospect of kissing other women wasn't very high, but at least the entire female population was in the realm of permissibility. But when I said "I do" to my wife, I was also saying "I can't" to kissing all those other women. (None of them have ever complained about this deprivation however.) The "do not touch" rule was immediately imposed, and that made all other women off limits to me.

I've remained sexually faithful to my wife during our marriage, but it hasn't been due to the power of the rule. Other rules don't compel my compliance (like speed limit laws), and the "do not touch" rule was equally unconvincing at times. But my love for my wife and for our kids was more than enough to motivate me to fidelity. Love, not the rule, compelled my loyalty to my wife.

And so it is in our relationship with God. Although we try diligently, the rules about sin don't always provide enough motivation for us. The pull of sin and temptation is too strong, and we're too weak. If we're trying to be faithful Christians on the basis of rule-keeping, we'll fail every time.

The proper spiritual motivation is somewhat counter-intuitive for us. We're accustomed to a cultural mind-set that says a positive mental attitude will solve all of society's ills. We tend to be motivated by incentives that provide results. We want more money, so we have a positive attitude about our finances. If we're unhappy about our employment situation, we're motivated to think positively about being on the career fast track. If we're unhappy with the lack of romance in our lives, we think positively about being a sexual magnet to the opposite gender. We'll do whatever we need to do to change our circumstances, and our self-interest provides the necessary motivation.

But that isn't how God intends for us to be motivated in our spiritual lives. He doesn't want us strategizing our Christian life from an egocentric perspective. Motivation is required for a Christian, but God's standard of motivation is on a higher plane and is more worthy than our own inflated self-interest.

To be sure, motivation is an essential component in the life of a Christian. We are called to be obedient followers of Christ, and that is not an easy assignment. As Jesus explained in the broadest sense, each of us must give up his or her life for Jesus' sake.[19] So discipleship has a cost. Our relationship with Christ is certainly worth the price, but you can't deny that the cost is difficult and sometimes painful. We don't want to be deterred by the cost and fall away, so we look for the motivation that will keep us faithful.

We can easily become disenchanted in our spiritual life when our motivation is inadequate to keep us energized and committed to the spiritual disciplines. For most of us, guilt is the motivator of choice. But it isn't effective for the long haul because we can become desensitized to guilt. Similarly, "because the Bible says so" is a popular but short-lived means of motivation for the reason that rule-keeping has no apparent intrinsic value for us. Avoiding guilt and keeping rules are not effective motivations because they are rooted in self-interest—how we feel about ourselves.

The only sustainable motivation is love. But not our love of self. Rather, our love for God should motivate us to conform our behaviors and attitudes to God's standards and remain faithful to him. Love transcends a mere mental commitment or intellectual ascent to the disciplines of the Christian life. Instead of operating out of forced compliance, we respond in love with conduct that we know is pleasing to the Lord. Motivation from a love for God finds us doing things because we know they bring joy to God. Thus we relieve ourselves of the notion that we're being forced to carry an oppressive burden. With love for God as our motivator, we aren't being forced to do anything; rather, we can choose to do what we know pleases God. That's a motivation that can keep us faithful.

⌒

Seeing God is difficult when our faith feels like a bunch of burdensome obligations. But we feel that way because we completely misunderstand the nature of Christian discipleship. God is pleased when he sees us living a Christlike lifestyle, but he isn't forcing rules and regulations on us to achieve it. He doesn't compel compliance to a spiritual checklist; rather, he extends grace to us. His forgiveness and grace should be our motivation. When we change our motivation, our vision of God will improve.

...Because the Bible Seems Irrelevant and Needs More About Me

That same day [when the women and disciples found Christ's tomb empty] two of Jesus' followers were walking to the village of Emmaus, seven miles from Jerusalem. As they walked along they were talking about everything that had happened. As they talked and discussed these things, Jesus himself suddenly came and began walking with them. But God kept them from recognizing him.

He asked them, "What are you discussing so intently as you walk along?"

They stopped short, sadness written across their faces. Then one of them, Cleopas, replied, "You must be the only person in Jerusalem who hasn't heard about all the things that have happened there the last few days."

"What things?" Jesus asked.

"The things that happened to Jesus, the man from Nazareth," they said. "He was a prophet who did powerful miracles, and he was a mighty teacher in the eyes of God and all the people. But our leading priests and other religious leaders handed him over to be condemned to death, and they crucified him. We had hoped he was the Messiah who had come to rescue Israel. This all happened three days ago.

"Then some women from our group of his followers were at his tomb early this morning, and they came back with an amazing report. They said his body was missing, and they had seen angels who told them Jesus is alive! Some of our men ran out to see, and sure enough, this body was gone, just as the women had said."

Then Jesus said to them, "You foolish people! You find it so hard to believe all that the prophets wrote in the Scriptures. Wasn't it clearly predicted that the Messiah would have to suffer all these things before entering his glory?" Then Jesus took them through the writings of Moses and all the prophets, explaining from all the Scriptures the things concerning himself.

By this time they were nearing Emmaus and the end of their journey. Jesus acted as if he were going on, but they begged him, "Stay the night with us, since it is getting late." So he went home with them. As they sat down to eat, he took the bread and blessed it. Then he broke it and gave it to them. Suddenly, their eyes were opened, and they recognized him. And at that moment he disappeared!

They said to each other, "Didn't our hearts burn within us as he talked with us on the road and explained the Scriptures to us?"[1]

Isn't that the sincere longing of almost every Christian—to have our hearts burn within us as God, through the Holy Spirit, illuminates the Scripture for us? Sadly, most of us go long intervals between such experiences, if we have them at all. Instead, we read the Scripture and find it dry and monotonous. Oh sure, we stumble upon some familiar nuggets in our reading that provide dependable encouragement (like Psalm 23 and 1 Corinthians 13), but most of what we read doesn't inspire us because it seems irrelevant to us. We know it shouldn't be that way. We don't want it to be that way. But the fact remains that the words on the page are just that—words on a page that appear unrelated to our daily lives.

But maybe the problem is not with the words but with our perspective as we read. When Christ explained the Scripture to those two disciples on the road to Emmaus, he explained "the things concerning *himself.*" He didn't elucidate the passages in a confined context of his listeners' self-interest. His explanations of scriptural teaching were centered on God, not on them.

Without a doubt, the Bible was written for us, but that doesn't mean that every verse is about us. We aren't the primary protagonists of the Bible; God is. Consequently, we shouldn't be reading the Bible to know more about ourselves but to discover more about God. We can easily get to the point where our hearts will burn within us every time we read Scripture, but the fuel for the fire will be a deeper understanding of God rather than an introspective search for ourselves.

∽

Bill Bright, the founder of Campus Crusade for Christ, developed an evangelistic tract in 1952 called *The Four Spiritual Laws.* The tract explains the essentials of the Christian faith concerning salvation. It begins with this first spiritual law: God loves you and offers a wonderful plan for your life.

That simple statement, premised squarely on John 3:16, refers to God's love for humanity and his plan to reconcile us with him so we can enjoy a relationship with him now and be present with him for eternity. Few people—other than atheists—quibbled about this statement when it was first published in 1952. But since then, the mind-set of our culture has shifted, and the first spiritual law might be a bit misleading to all who read it now—including Christians themselves.

A century or two ago our society acknowledged (at least in theory) the sovereignty of God, as evidenced by references to him in the Declaration of Independence, in the Pledge of Allegiance, and on our coins and currency. The cultural mind-set in those days included an almost unquestioned respect for biblical precepts. Details of theology were debated, of course, but overarching biblical concepts, such as the existence of God and the wisdom of the Ten Commandments, were almost universally accepted. People lived comfortably under the notion that God was large and in charge (at least on a metaphysical basis). So Bill Bright didn't stir up any controversy by issuing an explanation of God's existence and love for humanity.

But in the 50-plus years since Bill Bright penned *The Four Spiritual Laws,* our culture has drifted progressively away from such a broad-based application of Judeo-Christian precepts to our society. Now we're much more existential, adhering to a philosophy that views people as independent and completely responsible for their own actions, by which they make their own character.[2] We no longer recognize a single prevailing, controlling, authoritative voice (such as God or the Bible) that frames our theological and moral viewpoints as a society. Instead, individuals choose their own standards and framework for moral and theological issues. We don't even require people to articulate the evidence or logic of their viewpoint in this area. If they simply have an opinion, that's good enough. We're in an age when a belief system is considered legitimate simply because someone has a gut feeling about something. Call it gastrointestinal theology.

Christians haven't been insulated from this shift in the cultural mind-set. It has seeped into our thinking and tainted our theology. We twenty-first-century Christians continue to include God, the Bible, and church in the mix of our life components, but we tend to be influenced by a cultural perspective that makes us much more individualistic, relativistic, and narcissistic than our spiritual ancestors from the mid-twentieth century and earlier. In other words, we now read the first spiritual law and wonder how it benefits us rather than what it tells us about God.

Thanks in part to a segment of the Christian church that is guilty of marketing to the self-centered mentality of its membership and their unchurched neighbors, the context of the first spiritual law has changed. The "God loves you" part remains rooted in the theology of John 3:16, but the "and offers a wonderful plan for your life" part carries the suggestion of an individualized plan focused on personal satisfaction and fulfillment in the here and now. In other words, the first spiritual law, when read in the cultural context of an existential worldview, carries the connotation that God loves me and has an individualized plan to make me happy.

The Bible Tells Me No

You can understand why some churches are leaning toward a theology of an almighty God of the universe who wants to make us happy.[3] Who could resist the notion of an omnipotent deity who will orchestrate the circumstances and events of the universe for our own personal pleasure and prosperity? On a personal basis, we love the idea that God is going to cater to us. But this theology faces a gigantic problem: The Bible doesn't support it. A children's song says, "Yes, Jesus loves me; the Bible tells me so." Those lyrics are true, but the Bible does not say that his love for us means that he wants to put us at the center of our world. To that notion, the Bible says no.

Instead of an erroneous interpretation of the first spiritual law that has me at the center, the Bible presents a meta-narrative with a completely different focus. From Genesis to Revelation, we read of an overall, broad-reaching God-plan for humanity that has Christ at the center. This truly is the greatest story ever told. God intervening into human space and time to establish an intimate relationship with each of us is a story that I can get passionate about. It is something that can burn within me. It is a story worthy of our time, energy, and enthusiasm. But if we read the Bible from any other perspective, we'll have an inverted theology that keeps us from seeing God for who he is, for who he wants us to acknowledge him to be, and for what he desires to accomplish in our lives. Instead, we ourselves will be the main focus of the Bible with God as a supporting player rather than the other way around.

Look at the way the Bible tells the story of God implementing his plan through the ages: It is never about you or me as much as it is about him. And yes, the story includes specific guidelines and directives for how each of us as an individual is to live, but these are collective principals (for all of God's followers), not personalized and individualized agendas tailored for each individual person.

As God moved through history in the Old Testament, he used the nation of Israel as a representative of his care and direction for those who are reconciled to him. In the post-resurrection New Testament, God is using the church as his vehicle to draw us closer to him and to evangelize the lost. At Christ's return, he'll establish a restored kingdom for all of eternity. As Christ followers, we have a role in that God-designed strategy. But we are not the sine qua non to making it happen. Our lives are not at the epicenter of it all. In fact, we are called to give up our lives to Christ for the sake of his plan, which extends beyond us.

> Then Jesus said to his disciples, "If any of you wants to be my follower, you must turn from your selfish ways, take up your cross, and follow me. If you try to hang on to your life, you will lose it. But if you give up your life for my sake, you will save it."[4]

Rather than presenting a God who is preoccupied with our happiness, the Bible indicates that our personal meaning and satisfaction are by-products of God's overarching plan. We will experience our true purpose and happiness when we get on board with God's project of establishing his kingdom.

Who Is the Hero?

If we're looking for ourselves instead of God when we read the Bible, we'll twist and torture the meaning of the text every time—whether we do it consciously or unconsciously, and whether we're approaching the Word in humility or self-centeredness. For example, consider the familiar story of David and Goliath.

If I, as an adult Christian, read the Bible presupposing that I'm God's next spiritual hero (thanks to all that self-esteem my parents crammed into my cranium years ago), I'm going to find personal inspiration in the David and Goliath story. I'll see myself as God's obedient and unassuming servant, willing to walk onto the figurative battlefield. I'll be equipped with nothing except a slingshot and a bag of pebbles, and dressed in nothing more than a loincloth (again, speaking figuratively). But I'm willing to go against great odds for the sake of my Savior. I'll slay giants in his name. No obstacle is too great to deter my obedience to my heavenly Father. No form of terror that besets me can overcome my love for him. I am, by all accounts, a brave and devoted little follower of Christ, who will advance in spiritual battle while my Christian brothers stand quivering and sipping lattes in the church parking lot.

But the telling of my tale has me as the protagonist. I'm the hero. I give God a nod as I mention that my exploits are undertaken for his service, but when I play this story on the IMAX movie screen of my mind, I am in the starring role, and God makes only a cameo appearance.

In the real David and Goliath story, David was not the hero. If I am looking for God in the story, I'll quickly see that David is the supporting actor to God's starring role. David himself said that the battle and victory were the Lord's: "Today the LORD will conquer you...The whole world will know that there is a God in Israel! And everyone assembled here will know that the Lord rescues his people...This is the Lord's battle, and he will give you to us!"[5]

If I'm reading a passage looking for God, I'll find him. I won't find much to divert my focus away from God and onto me. But if I read the same passage making it all about me, I will find very little about God (although I'm sure he's somewhere, hiding in the shadow of my magnificence).

The Bible Tells Me So

If we approach the Bible from a narcissistic point of view, expecting to find ourselves in the pivotal role of God's story, we can make almost any text about ourselves. But most of us aren't so self-deluded that we hope to read our names in the acknowledgments page at the front of the Bible. We wouldn't go so far as to say that God couldn't have done it without our help. No, our egotism doesn't take us that far. But it does pervert the way we read and understand what the Bible says about God.

The classical study of literature in the past focused on what the *author* intended to say. Gradually, in the twentieth century, the focus shifted to what the *text* itself said. (Most of the authors were pushing up daisies, so they weren't around for comment. You could draw your meaning from the words of the text, and the *author* couldn't contradict you.) But with the recent emphasis on self-esteem and self-realization, the contemporary study of literature in our educational system has become reader-centric: What does the story or essay mean to *you*? The actual intention of the author becomes almost irrelevant because the individual reader's own opinion is prized so highly.

When we study the Bible with this "What does it mean to *me?*" approach, we become the arbiter of what we read. We subconsciously elevate ourselves above God because we determine for ourselves the meaning of the text rather than looking for the meaning that God intended.

Lots of Bible study aids reinforce this perverted perception. These Bible study guides were appropriate and effective when they were written, but now, decades later, they cater to what has become our existential and narcissistic inclination. For example, many Bible teachers (including me) have recommended this three-step approach to understanding a passage from Scripture:

- *Observation.* Ask yourself, *What does the passage say?* This involves actually reading the passage, which is a pretty good way to start. (Some people want to opine about a Bible passage or teaching of Jesus without even reading it. Amazing.) This is when you look in the text for people's names and emotions, cause-and-effect relationships, lists, comparisons and contrasts, and the like.

- *Interpretation.* Ask yourself, *What does the passage mean?* Now we're getting into a little extra-credit work. This step usually requires examining the broader context in which the passage is written. Do any chronological, geographical, biographical, cultural, or archaeological references bring meaning to the passage? Does the passage use hyperbole, or was it written to be taken literally? Does the teaching of this passage appear to be consistent with the rest of Scripture? If it appears to be contrary to other parts of the Bible, you may want to rinse and repeat.

- *Application.* Ask yourself, *What does this passage mean to me?* This is where we get personal, asking how God wants to transform us in light of what we have read. When we bump face-to-face into biblical truth, we usually need to respond in some way. Maybe the passage calls for greater devotion to God; maybe it encourages change in our lifestyle. Applying Scripture to our life involves obedience to God by following what the Holy Spirit teaches us from God's Word.

Here's the rub. Without an adequate explanation of the application step, any self-respecting existentialist would salivate at the prospect of deciding for herself or himself the substance of a passage. That is why the question, what does it mean to me? has become dangerous when tossed loosely into small-group Bible studies. Instead of finding an application that involves a description of life transformation based on a well-researched interpretation of the passage, folks might simply share their uninformed but supposedly valid interpretations, chat about several disparate opinions, and select one as God's truth for them.

The Hard Work of Bible Reading

Of course, we cannot abandon reading our Bible simply because the process is fraught with dangers of self-centered interpretation. Just as milk is essential for an infant's growth, God's Word is essential to our spiritual growth. "Like newborn babies, you must crave pure spiritual milk so that you will grow into a full experience of salvation."[6]

Yet many of us are content to remain spiritual babies. We like the taste of milk, and no chewing is required. Milk goes down easy, but solid food requires mastication and digestion—both of which come at the inconvenience of time and effort. Being a baby Christian is easy, but God wants us to grow out of it.

> There is much more we would like to say about this, but it is difficult to explain, especially since you are spiritually dull and don't seem to listen. You have been believers so long now that you ought to be teaching others. Instead, you need someone to teach you again the basic things about God's word. You are like babies who need milk and cannot eat solid food. For someone who lives on milk is still an infant and doesn't know how to do what is right. Solid food is for those who are mature, who through training have the skill to recognize the difference between right and wrong.[7]

To move from spiritual infancy to maturity, we must appropriate God's truth as revealed through Scripture.

> You have been taught the holy Scriptures from childhood, and they have given you the wisdom to receive the salvation that comes by trust in Christ Jesus. All Scripture is inspired by God and is useful to teach us what is true and to make us realize what is wrong in our lives. It corrects us when we are wrong and teaches us to do what is right. God uses it to prepare and equip his people to do every good work.[8]

The Bible provides everything we need: doctrine, conviction, correction, and direction. But we receive all of that only when we read in reverence for the Author and with no agenda to make ourselves the major players in God's plan.

⌒

Without a doubt, the Bible is not an easy book to read. More correctly, it is just as easy to read as any other book, but it is more difficult to understand than most. Many passages take considerable effort to understand. We shouldn't feel bad (about ourselves or God) if a first reading seems irrelevant. But if we're not seeing the connection between the passage and our lives, we might be looking for what the passage is saying about us and missing what it's saying about God.

God's prominence in Scripture is much easier to see when we are reading with the right motivation. There is a direct correlation between the way we approach the Bible and what we get out of it.

Some of us read the Bible because we feel guilty or obligated. We have to do it because we've been told we have to do it. When we read this way, we usually see God in Scripture as a tough taskmaster.

Others of us read the Bible because we feel proud about how much we know. We want to be able to spout out whatever Bible verse is necessary to win an argument; we want to fill our head with knowledge about God so we can appear spiritual to ourselves and to others. When we read this way, we treat the Bible like a textbook and often miss the heart of God in Scripture.

The Bible invites a different kind of reader—one who reads for the sake of Spirit-prompted transformation. That was David's desire: "I have hidden your word in my heart, that I might not sin against you...Your word is a lamp to guide my feet and a light for my path."[9]

The verses in Scripture will reflect the appropriate relationship between God and us if we read them in the correct context. There will be no question about who is the major player and who has the subservient role. When we open the Bible with that perspective in mind, we'll have no problem clearly seeing God.

LETTING SCRIPTURE SPEAK FOR ITSELF

The Gospels are filled with examples of people who saw Jesus face-to-face, heard his words, and walked away changed forever by the encounter. Others, however, also met Christ, heard his words, and walked away unaffected. In most cases, the difference has to do with the way the person responded to the words he or she heard. Those who heard the words and took them to heart were changed forever. Tragically, those who ignored or disregarded what Christ said couldn't even comprehend the magnitude of their missed opportunity.

I suspect that you want to be changed forever. Even beyond the consequence of your salvation, you want to experience the abundant life that Christ promised in John 10:10. You aren't likely to see Christ in person during your earthly lifetime, but you still have the opportunity of encountering him through the words he spoke while teaching in and around Jerusalem approximately 2000 years ago. You can read verbatim the words he spoke to others whose lives were transformed by what they heard.

The words of Christ (as well as the rest of Scripture) can be as life-changing or as unheeded today as they were 2000 years ago. The outcome will depend on what you do with what you read.

⸺

We live in a world geared for instant gratification, so many of us don't take the time to study Bible verses as well as we should. We find one that sounds good, is meaningful to us, and is memorable. It becomes our go-to verse in times of trouble. But we do ourselves a disfavor—and God is disrespected—when we're more concerned with how the verse sounds than what it really means.

We violate God's Word whenever we take a verse out of context. It may sound good all by itself, but its apparent meaning is incorrect or is misleading when the verse lacks the proper contextual meaning. Check out this favorite: "Delight yourself in the LORD, and he will give you the desires of your heart."[10]

All by itself, this verse could be read to mean that if you enjoy the Lord, he will give you whatever you want. A more mature understanding of God—based on more familiarity with Scripture—doesn't put God in the role of a genie responding to our wishes. Instead, it reveals that people who are in close fellowship with God will have desires that grow out of his nature. In other words, a sincere and mature Christian will have the desires that God germinates. So God doesn't give us whatever we desire, but he will give us our desires. It is a fine distinction that has tremendous theological impact for our lives. If we misunderstand the verse (and put our hopes on that incorrect interpretation), we can be disappointed in God for failing to do what we thought the verse promised.

Just as a few words can be misunderstood, so too can the meaning of a verse be lost without the proper context of the surrounding passage. Take this statement made by the apostle Paul: "I can do everything through Christ, who gives me strength."[11]

This verse has universal appeal. Whether you're an athlete in training for the Olympics, a politician hoping to be elected to public office, or a diminutive author hoping to be taller, you can quote this verse as inspiration and God's promise for your situation. More precisely, you can *misquote* this verse for your situation. Although the words may seem to say so, this is not a promise that you can do everything if Christ is in you.

The context of this verse is Paul's explanation about spiritual contentment. The Christians in the church at Philippi wanted to send him some financial assistance. He appreciated their gesture, but he wanted them to know that his living situation was irrelevant to his spiritual outlook. Notice how the meaning of the verse changes when read in the context of the entire passage:

> How I praise the Lord that you are concerned about me again. I know you have always been concerned for me, but you didn't have the chance to help me. Not that I was ever in need, for I have learned how to be content with whatever I have. I know how to live on almost nothing or with everything. I have learned the secret of living in every situation, whether it is with a full stomach or empty, with plenty or little. For I can do everything through Christ, who gives me strength. Even so, you have done well to share with me in my present difficulty.[12]

Of course, even taken out of context, the verse is correct because God is omnipotent and can accomplish all things. If he wants to make me president of the United States or help me qualify for the U.S. Olympic team, he can make it happen. (Apparently the only thing he flat-out refuses to do is make me taller.) But God's omnipotence isn't the proposition of the verse. Rather, Paul was stating his spiritual perspective, which is influenced by neither lavish nor austere circumstances. And for us to quote the verse as a promise for victory that is applicable in all situations might lead us to think that God hasn't been faithful to his Word when our expectation of what he will do doesn't match with reality.

If we are serious about getting to know God better, we need to do a better job of learning to read God's Word for what it really says.

⌒

Our ability to see God clearly is hindered if we're expecting him to be something other than what he really is. Scripture contains plenty of beautiful descriptions of his character. We must read his Word correctly so our view of him is not obscured by our misinterpretation of Scripture.

...Because I'm Too Concerned with Being Happy

I live on the edge. Not at the edge of danger and not on the edge in an extreme sports kind of way. I'm an author, not an action hero kind of guy. But I'm always on the edge of my ability to keep life under control. I'm usually somewhere not too far from the end of my rope. The frayed end, where the strands are unraveling.

This is true of many of us. Our lives are too hectic, too full, and too tiring. At the end of the evening, if I can manage to stay awake for a few moments in bed, I talk to God about it. I commiserate with God about my plight, being careful not to blame him for my circumstances, but praying for a divine extraction from them. I never ask, *Where did I go wrong?* because I'm afraid of hearing him reply, *This is gonna take more than one night.* But I often find myself saying something like, *Lord, I just want to be happy. And I know you want me to be happy too, right?* Or at least that is what I used to say, before I realized that God is using a different definition of the term "happy."

The New Testament book of Colossians is a Bible study favorite for a lot of Christians. The cynics among us might say that Colossians is popular because it only has four chapters. Granted, four chapters are easier to digest than the sixty-six chapters of Isaiah, or the one hundred fifty chapters of Psalms. But many of us have a fondness for Colossians that transcends its brevity.

Sound like Anyone You Know?

A sense of relevance permeates Colossians more than some other epistles. Paul talks about practical aspects of relationships (like marriage, family, and work) and the struggle of living a holy life. But beyond the obvious preference for practical theology, Colossians attracts us because Paul seems to be talking directly to *us* and not to some ragtag group of fledgling Christians. This subtle appeal arises from a cultural context that we share in common with Paul's Colossian audience.

Paul was writing to Christians who were living in one of the cultural hotspots of the first century. The citizens of Colosse were primarily a sophisticated, affluent, highly educated group. They were the hipsters of their day, on the leading edge of every social trend. Sound familiar? Even though we twenty-first-century Christians are supposed to be in the world but not of the world,[1] we're pretty much riding the wave that sets the trends for the world. Along with the rest of our Western society, we pride ourselves in being conversant in all cultural touchpoints. We know our Hollywood and sports celebrities (as well or better than we know the Old Testament patriarchs), we Tivo the "must watch" television shows, and we recognize the names of couture designers (thanks to product lines that have infiltrated the masses with merchandise at Costco and Lowe's stores). Yep, we're just like the Colossians, only 2000 years later.

And that similarity is exactly why we need to heed words of

warning written by Paul to the Colossians: "In him [Christ] lie hidden all the treasures of wisdom and knowledge. I am telling you this so no one will deceive you with well-crafted arguments."[2]

It probably came as no shock to the Colossians that Christ was the repository of all wisdom and knowledge. They'd heard that from Paul before. But they might have taken offense when Paul implied that they were susceptible to being misled by false teaching. Let's be honest about it. Most of us think we're intellectually savvy and spiritually mature enough to recognize false teaching when we hear it. But that's Paul's point exactly. We think we're so smart and so culturally hip that we'll be able to detect erroneous philosophies. But we may be fooled when they come to us subtly, wrapped in the guise of a cultural mind-set.

The Relentless Pursuit of Happiness

Consider happiness, for example. This is a concept we're familiar with, more or less. And few of us would think that anything about happiness is spiritually subversive. I know I didn't—until I heard a lecture on the subject by Dr. J.P. Moreland and was motivated to read his book about it.[3] Moreland contends that our culture is becoming obsessed with happiness. We're addicted to the relentless pursuit of it. And as a result, we are becoming unhappier as individuals. He calls it the paradox of hedonism—the more you try to become happy, the less happy you'll become in the process.

Like any respectable philosophy professor (and he is a highly regarded one), Dr. Moreland has data to back up his contention. In his book he summarizes the research studies of Paul Campos at the University of Colorado and of Martin Seligman from the University of Pennsylvania. Here's a synopsis of Moreland's summary.

Campos concludes that we are richer, healthier, more youthful, and safer than our ancestors of only 50 years ago. Although the American dream of being better off than your parents is coming true for many people, Americans are not getting happier. In fact, Americans are less happy than they have ever been. The percentage of the population that considers itself "very unhappy" is increasing by 20 percent with each generation.

Seligman found that the incidence of depression has increased ten times in the span of one generation (the Baby Boomers). He says the Boomers stopped trying to live for something bigger than themselves (unlike their parents of the World War II generation, which has been dubbed "the greatest generation" for its self-sacrifice for family and country). The Boomers started living for their own personal and private happiness, which according to Seligman is a recipe for depression. Seligman concludes that the American dream is based on a mistaken view of life—delivered through the media—that increasing levels of wealth and health will produce increasing levels of happiness.

Moreland explains these outcomes as the consequences of a diametric change in our definition of happiness. The traditional notion of happiness was around for about 2500 years, but it has been replaced by a contemporary view of happiness since the 1950s (coinciding, not surprisingly, with the emergence of the self-centered Boomer Generation).

Contemporary Happiness

The concept of contemporary happiness is simpler (and shallower), so let's start with that. Webster's New College Dictionary defines happiness as a sense of pleasurable satisfaction. It is an intense emotion or feeling that occurs inside of us. External forces affect this type of happiness. That's why we say that something makes us happy.

This is good news and bad news. The good news is that contemporary happiness is a feel-good experience. It will put a smile on your face. The bad news is that it doesn't last for long. It is transitory and fleeting. Happy today, glum tomorrow. So you have to go searching for more of the next thing that will give you the intense feeling that has since worn off. This leads to an endless quest to stay in a state of happiness.

Who are the role models of a lifestyle built on contemporary happiness? They are the celebrities who are famous only for being famous, the ones whose only distinction is the excessiveness of their partying, the ones who will be tabloid fodder during their next crash-and-burn episode (the inevitable downturn between happiness highs).

Classical Happiness

In contrast, the classical view of happiness refers to a life well lived. Classical happiness is a result of a life of virtue and character, a life that manifests wisdom, kindness, and goodness. Unlike contemporary happiness, classical happiness is not premised on emotions, feelings, or external circumstances. It is found in the substance of a quality life.

This is the definition of happiness that Moses, Plato, and Aristotle assumed. It is what the unknown Israelite writer had in mind when he penned the story of Job's sufferings: "Happy is the man whom God correcteth: therefore despise not thou the chastening of the Almighty."[4]

Job knew a thing or two about tough times, and whether they were initiated by God's correction or Satan's wager, Job had a macro-view of life that allowed him to see those circumstances as beneficial. He was happy—not in the sense of being giddy with excitement over his boils, his financial losses, and the windstorm that killed all his children, but happy in the knowledge that God was at work in his life.

Classical happiness is at the core of many of the proverbs, which recognize that spiritual wisdom is the predicate to a life that flourishes with virtue and nobility: "Happy is the man that findeth wisdom, and the man that getteth understanding."[5]

The classical definition is what the signers of the Declaration of Independence had in mind when they subscribed to "life, liberty, and the pursuit of happiness" as inalienable rights. They were not claiming the right to always experience pleasurable satisfaction, but rather claiming the right to pursue a life of integrity and uprightness.

This type of happiness is internalized in your personal belief systems, so it tends to be much stabler and more permanent than contemporary happiness. It becomes integrated into your personality and actually serves as a guiding principal in your life.

And what about contemporary role models who display classical happiness? Rather than being mere celebrities, the people who embody classical happiness are heroes in the truest sense. They are willing to sacrifice themselves for the good of others. These are often unsung heroes who may never be famous. You're not likely to see them on the cover of *People* magazine because they don't seek out publicity. They are volunteers in your community and in your church; they are teachers who accept substandard pay for the joy of building the lives of their students; they are the cadre of young adults who commit their time to advancing the cause of social justice around the globe on behalf of the poor and powerless.

Which Would You Prefer?

When you dissect and analyze happiness as Moreland has done, you come away with a clear winner. The triviality of contemporary happiness pales in comparison to the substance and quality of classical happiness. So classical happiness must be the goal of any rationally thinking person, right? You know better than that. We've done exactly what Paul warned the Colossians about. We've been deceived and led astray by a smooth, fine-sounding cultural philosophy of happiness. We're going for what is superficial and missing what has true value.

Sadly, this societal mind-set has infected people who by all measures are usually pretty reliable sources for advice. I'm referring to your parents. They may be wise in most other matters, but their thinking is corrupted on this issue. Once you have reached the point of being off all parental subsidies, they seem uncharacteristically open-minded: "I don't care how much money you make, the size of your house, or the kind of car you drive. I just want you to be *happy*." They think that's an admirable attitude on their part—they're showing that they've outgrown the symbols of success that were important to their generation, and they don't want you to get caught up in the rat race of conspicuous consumption that plagued the Boomers. But a goal of shallow, meaningless, fleeting contemporary happiness is a pathetic parental aspiration for one's child. We should want something nobler and more virtuous for ourselves and our children. We should be pursing classical happiness.

What Does Christ Know About Happiness?

Jesus didn't use the word "happiness," but he had the notion of classical happiness in mind when he preached the Sermon on the Mount. It doesn't violate the text to substitute "happy" (in the classical sense) in place of "blessed" each time it occurs in the following verses:

> Blessed are the poor in spirit, for theirs is the kingdom
> of heaven.
> Blessed are those who mourn, for they will be comforted.
> Blessed are the meek, for they will inherit the earth.
> Blessed are those who hunger and thirst for righteousness,
> for they will be filled.
> Blessed are the merciful, for they will be shown mercy.
> Blessed are the pure in heart, for they will see God.
> Blessed are the peacemakers, for they will be called sons
> of God.
> Blessed are those who are persecuted because of righteous-
> ness, for theirs is the kingdom of heaven.
> Blessed are you when people insult you, persecute you and
> falsely say all kinds of evil against you because of me.[6]

The people to whom Christ refers in this passage are happy—in the classical definition—not because of their external circumstances, but because they don't have a self-centered perspective on life itself. At its heart, Christian discipleship presupposes classical happiness. Christ goes so far as to say that self-denial, not self-gratification, will be the source of happiness for his followers (although he didn't exactly use the "h" word):

> Then Jesus said to his disciples, "If any of you wants to be my follower, you must turn from your selfish ways, take up your cross, and follow me. If you try to hang on to your life, you will lose it. But if you give up your life for my sake, you will save it."[7]

Jesus is inviting his followers to eternal life, but what good is eternity if you're miserable the entire time? That's the fantastic news about Christ's eternity—it is a combo deal with an "abundant life" in the here and now and in the everlasting ending that follows. The John 10:10 life that Jesus offers is one of classical happiness—a life that is overflowing in quality and character. You won't always be giggly happy, but you can live in the "true meaning in life" kind of happiness.

The Christian life offered by Christ—much like classical happiness—seems counterintuitive to our modern culture, which revels in personal pleasure. Christ is all about the substance of your inner life, not the trappings of your external life, which we foolishly equate with being happy. Spiritual principles are at play in all of this, and Christ knew that his thick-skulled disciples (ourselves included) might not be able to absorb the concept in the abstract. But we can learn it by example, and that's what Christ gave us—the personal example of his death on the cross. "Take up your cross and follow me" would just be a catchy motto for Christianity if it weren't accompanied by the horror of his actual crucifixion. But with the mental picture of Christ hanging in agony on the cross, we can start to understand that denying ourselves, taking up our crosses, and following Jesus isn't going to put us in the realm of contemporary happiness.

Of course, as a general rule, Jesus isn't asking us to actually die on a cross (although in some parts of the world martyrdom for the sake of Christ *is* the general rule). He is not referring primarily to an action, but to an attitude. "Deny yourself and take up your cross" describes a worldview in which we advance God's kingdom instead of our own selfish interests. We want and work for what he wants because we know it pleases him and is best for our world and for ourselves. Knowing that we're part of his divine solution for humankind puts us smack-dab in the center of classical happiness.

Finding the Balance

Fulfilling the challenge to deny ourselves and take up our crosses requires a fine balance. With that as our orientation, we can leave the external circumstances to Christ. He is not mandating that we live without enjoyment or wealth. He is not advocating asceticism. So we can work and earn a living, save and invest, and spend money on ourselves within the bounds of good stewardship. In other words, we are not required to don a pith helmet and trek to the Gobi hinterland, where we will be isolated from even the smallest pleasures of life (although Wal-Mart soon may be opening a store there).

"Deny yourself and take up your cross" is not an invitation to self-deprivation. It is about having a perspective that transcends any notion that happiness is equated with prosperity. We may have some of the trappings that the world considers essential for contemporary happiness, but these are just temporal blessings that God may choose to bestow. Our happiness is in him, not in the stuff. So whether we have the stuff or don't have the stuff is irrelevant to our hold on happiness.

Paul's warning is applicable on both ends of the spectrum. We need to be wary of the cultural take on happiness and not let it infect our spiritual mind-set. Likewise, we need to resist the reactionary theology that condemns fun and enjoyment under the guise of denying yourself.

What You're Looking for Affects What You'll See

So we see a great divide between classical happiness and contemporary happiness. If you're looking for happiness or expecting Christ to bring it to you, you should know which definition you're using.

Your perspective about happiness influences your spiritual sensitivity. If you're operating from a position of contemporary happiness, you'll be expecting God's will to include nothing but good times. You'll be sorely disappointed when you find yourself in a period of prolonged adversity. You'll be saying, *Lord, I just want to be happy, so why do you keep putting me in circumstances where I have to pick up a cross?* On the other hand, if your understanding of happiness has you ready and willing to pick up that cross in the advance of God's kingdom in your own network of family, friends, and business relationships, you won't be disappointed when the spiritual going gets tough.

Your mind-set on this happiness issue also affects the way you read Scripture. Are you reading the Bible and looking for passages that make you happy (contemporary version), or are you realizing true happiness in what you read (classic definition)? The dichotomy is illustrated in a verse like this: "We know that God causes everything to work together for the good of those who love God and are called according to his purpose for them."[8]

Your understanding of the spiritual underpinnings of this verse will depend on your worldview of happiness. It all turns on how you interpret the "good" that will eventually befall those who follow after God. Does your understanding leave you feeling lightheaded with the expectation of emotional happiness, or does it allow you to see and appreciate that somehow your travail has worked to further the kingdom of God?

Being Happy with the Cross

Taking up the cross sounds like a horrendous task, and intuitively it seems far from anything associated with happiness. But reprogramming ourselves to understand happiness in its classical sense can make the rough road we walk when following Christ seem less intimidating. A sense of classical happiness in our lives will make the weight of the cross we carry seem lighter. The obstacles in our journey will no longer seem insurmountable. The substance of God's true happiness in our lives will make the burdens of following Christ more bearable. And maybe that's what Jesus was talking about when he uttered the oxymoronic statement of Christian discipleship: "For my yoke is easy to bear, and the burden I give you is light."[9]

He isn't saying that our spiritual journey will be hassle free. But he is promising that by his spirit, we can experience happiness in the difficulties.

As it turns out, I'm back to praying each night for more happiness in my life. Nothing is wrong with me wanting to be happy. In fact, it is a good thing. Moreover, that is what God wants for me too. But now he and I are simpatico on the definition. It's a happiness rooted in denying myself, taking up my cross, and following Christ. It is a happiness that grows out of advancing God's agenda for the world and for my life. It is a happiness that culminates in finding myself as a part of his divine plan. And that puts me to sleep with a smile on my face.

Getting a Glimpse of God

BRINGING EXHORTATION INTO YOUR LIFE

In my professional life, I've had mentors and even a life coach. I always enjoyed these relationships because they stretched me a bit, and I usually needed the accountability. I always felt I was making progress. I didn't always agree with what my mentors suggested, but I always considered what they said because I respected them.

In my spiritual life, I haven't been as fortunate to have mentors (probably because I didn't seek them out). From time to time I've been in small groups, and I enjoyed these relationships, but they never seemed to produce the progress that I found in my occupational mentoring. Perhaps it was because I never had a real spiritual mentor. I always hung around one or more guys pretty much just like me. None of us had the spiritual gravitas to make the rest of us pay close attention. We didn't always seriously consider what was being said because the guy who said it was just as messed up as the rest of us.

A little more than a year ago I began the search for a spiritual mentor. As I developed a profile for the kind of guy I was looking for, it started to look a lot like the apostle Paul. Then I wondered, *Hey, what about Paul?* Oh sure, this pairing would include some mentoring challenges. We come from fairly diverse societal settings, and then we'd have to deal with the fact that Paul is dead. But those two minor complications didn't make the relationship impossible. In fact, I've been having fairly regular mentoring sessions with Paul every Tuesday morning at Starbucks for almost a year. I make these appointments a priority. I grab a coffee and sit at a table and read a passage from one of his epistles. Then I ask myself, *What is God, through the words of Paul, trying to coach me on today?* Then I reread the passage. The entire session takes less than an hour. It has turned out to be some of the best spiritual mentoring I've ever had. It's more than just a casual discussion between the two of us. That guy really knows how to motivate me to get serious in my relationship with God.

Plenty of people are usually available to help us when we are young in our faith. The pastor delivers weekly sermons, teachers in the church's children program care for our little ones, and we can always find a small-group leader or a Bible study leader if we choose to. But once you get past the teaching of the basics of the Christian faith, the learning curve starts to flatten out. This is when many of us pull back a little and cut ourselves off from any spiritual accountability. Ironically, this is exactly the point at which we need someone in our lives who can take spiritual principles and insights (that we already know) and apply them directly and specifically to our spiritual quirks and deficiencies (that we've been overlooking).

As I've gotten maturer in my faith, I've assumed responsibility for discipling others in their Christian walk. But I've neglected to engage the help of someone who can continue my spiritual tutelage. Watching some of the great Bible teachers on TV doesn't count, nor does listening to podcasts of good sermons. These preachers and Bible teachers don't know me. They can speak God's truth, but I can pretty quickly hit the off switch and avoid any uncomfortable and convicting confrontation with the Holy Spirit.

Nope, conviction by means of technology lacks accountability. I need someone who will get up close and personal with me; someone who will get in my face. I need a personal exhorter.

God's design for Christianity includes a role for someone who knows us well enough to challenge us in our faith in appropriate and necessary ways. "Exhort one another day by day, so long as it is called Today, lest any one of you be hardened by the deceitfulness of sin."[10]

The word "exhort" has fallen out of our contemporary lexicon, and maybe that's why Eugene Peterson translated it as "keep each other on your toes" in *The Message* paraphrase of that verse. The Greek word used by the writer of Hebrews is *parakaleo*. It has a full and broad meaning that covers such English words as these: admonish, encourage, urge, rebuke, console, beseech, warn, comfort, and plead.

Exhortation, in the spiritual sense, is one Christian pleading with another to get his or her life right with Christ. The obstacle at issue may be a small one or a large one. Either way, it is an obstacle that is interfering with a Christian brother or sister's relationship with Christ, and that is never a good thing and must never be ignored. So our responsibility to exhort one another carries more *urgency* than the mere whining of a child pestering a parent for a glass of water at bedtime. And it carries a *greater expectation for compliance* than the hope of a panhandler who is being disregarded by pedestrians passing by. At the heart of exhortation is a sense that our spiritual well-being is at risk unless we heed the words that are being spoken.

As a general rule, Christians aren't into exhortation that much. Our problem is not that we don't see spiritual failings and danger signals in our Christian friends' lives. We see them easily enough, but we usually don't have a close enough relationship with our friends to entitle us to talk about the issues. Furthermore, even if we have a close friendship that permits such openness, we don't want to say anything even remotely critical because then we're leaving ourselves vulnerable for reciprocation (the spiritual way to say "retaliation"). In other words, I'm not going to say anything spiritually confrontational to you, not because you don't need to hear it, but because I don't want to open myself up to letting you take spiritual potshots at me (that I actually need to hear).

So as friends, we let each other walk on the edge of the precipice because saying nothing is more comfortable than shouting a warning.

⌒

If we want to get serious about knowing God better and seeing him more clearly, we better heed his instructions for doing so. According to his directives, we need to be so intimately involved with a group of other Christians that we can exhort one another. We need to be encouraged and admonished and consoled and motivated by each other in our spiritual walk.

We need to be doing with other Christians exactly what the apostle Paul was doing with the Christians in those fledging first-century churches. This requires committed friendships that are premised on authenticity and vulnerability for the sake of our relationships with Christ and each other. When we get to that place, we can actually have a real living person who will sit across from us at Starbucks and whom God can use as his spokesperson for the spiritual mentoring we need.

...Because I
Missed the
First 37 Years
of Eternity

Even though I was a kid when I became a Christian, the whole salvation thing seemed like a no-brainer. From my pint-sized vantage point, it didn't appear to take a genius (or even an adult) to see the wisdom in accepting Christ as my personal Savior. Look at the two mutually exclusive options that were presented to me: Either (a) I turn my life over to Christ and accept him as my Lord and Savior, and then I'll spend eternity with him in heaven, or (b) I live for myself while I'm alive on earth, but then after I'm dead I'll spend all of eternity in pain and anguish as I burn in hell. Hmmm... So as a little kid, I reasoned it out this way: Getting a ticket to heaven seems like the safest bet, especially because I can still sin whenever I want and God's grace and forgiveness will cover me. (Little kids are particularly adept at finding the loopholes.) Yep, even as a child I could see that option (a) was the only choice that made sense.

So before the onset of puberty, I became a Christian. My life as a Christian kid wasn't too much different from my non-Christian friends' lives. It consisted basically of doing kid stuff, with the only distinction that my activities were within the parameters allowed by my parents' brand of Christianity. For example, my parents were big on supporting missionaries, and I remember having a world map in my room with the equivalent of missionary trading cards stapled around the edge of the map. I had drawn lines from each missionary's card to the country where the missionary lived. This missionary display was eventually dismantled and replaced by a series of major league baseball posters. (I still prayed for the missionaries, but I was relieved that I would no longer have to explain the map to any friends who came over to my house to play.)[1]

My burgeoning faith included some daily activities (praying at meals and bedtime, reading the Bible, and having devotions on a somewhat regular basis). But my predominate Christian activity as a kid was waiting: waiting for eternity to begin.

Figuratively speaking, when I became a Christian, I put my "go to heaven free" ticket in my underwear drawer for safekeeping and went on with life, knowing I'd need it when eternity arrived. The exact date for the commencement of eternity was unknown to me, but I knew it would be triggered by either of two events: my death or the return of Christ, whichever came first. I didn't know when either of those incidents would occur, but I assumed that they'd happen sometime way out in the future when I was old and decrepit—like age 57. In the early 1970s, a few Bible-thumping evangelists predicted a narrow window in the time-space continuum for Christ's return, so for a while I was thinking I'd be using my ticket any day, but all of these predictions turned out to be bogus. So by college, my ticket was in the underwear drawer of my mind, tucked away for safekeeping and future reference along with other things I had committed to memory, like my Social Security number and my gym locker combination. As the years went by, I added other important items to remember, like my wife's birthday and the names of our two children.

All in all, I spent the first 37 years of my Christian life waiting for eternity to begin. Imagine my surprise when I came to the shocking realization that it had started 37 years earlier, and I had missed it.

∽

A church in my town has a different cheesy Christian slogan on its marquee every week. No one person could think of all of these hokey evangelistic maxims, so there must be a book that has a compilation of them. You probably know exactly what I'm talking about; sayings like "Life got you frowning? Maybe it's time for a faith lift." Or "There are two sections in eternity: smoking and non-smoking." And who can forget (although I'm trying hard to), "It's Adam and Eve, not Adam and Steve."

I'm not a big fan of signs like these because the slogans are usually a combination of bad jokes, poor theology, and a writing style that sounds self-righteous or condescending. I don't mean to go on a rant about this, but I have in my mind a marquee message of several weeks ago: "Christians need an optometrist because we're all cross-eyed." Like most of these ecclesiastical one-liners, that statement contains a bit of truth, although you might miss it because it is camouflaged by the weak witticism.

Our Bifurcated Vision

Our salvation is rooted in Christ's sacrificial death on the cross, where he paid the ultimate penalty for our sin. Accordingly, we look back in time to that late afternoon on the hillside at Golgotha and see a clear picture of Christ on the cross. We need to have that image emblazoned in our memories. That event is pivotal in our salvation and is foundational for our faith, so the writers of the epistles frequently reminded the first-century Christians of Christ's death on the cross. It is a reccurring touchpoint in each of the epistles. Here are nine examples from nine different New Testament letters:

- For since our friendship with God was restored by the death of his Son while we were still his enemies, we will certainly be saved through the life of his Son.[2]

- The message of the cross is foolish to those who are headed for destruction! But we who are being saved know it is the very power of God.[3]

- Christ has rescued us from the curse pronounced by the law. When he was hung on the cross, he took upon himself the curse for our wrongdoing.[4]

- Christ himself has brought peace to us. He united Jews and Gentiles into one people when, in his own body on the cross, he broke down the wall of hostility that separated us...Together as one body, Christ reconciled both groups to God by means of his death on the cross, and our hostility toward each other was put to death.[5]

- He humbled himself in obedience to God and died a criminal's death on a cross.[6]

- Through him God reconciled everything to himself. He made peace with everything in heaven and on earth by means of Christ's blood on the cross.[7]

- We do this by keeping our eyes on Jesus, the champion who initiates and perfects our faith. Because of the joy awaiting him, he endured the cross, disregarding its shame.[8]

- He personally carried our sins in his body on the cross so that we can be dead to sin and live for what is right. By his wounds you are healed.[9]

- Jesus Christ was revealed as God's Son by his baptism in water and by shedding his blood on the cross—not by water only, but by water and blood.[10]

Reminders like these provide a strong biblical mandate for us to keep the work of Christ on the cross as a continual focus in our faith.

We need to look back at the cross to remember what Christ did for us, but we are also encouraged throughout the epistles to look forward with expectancy to Christ's imminent and triumphant return. These verses are also all from different New Testament letters:

- Now you have every spiritual gift you need as you eagerly wait for the return of our Lord Jesus Christ.[11]

- We are citizens of heaven, where the Lord Jesus Christ lives. And we are eagerly waiting for him to return as our Savior.[12]

- Christ died for us so that, whether we are dead or alive when he returns, we can live with him forever.[13]

- Now the prize awaits me—the crown of righteousness, which the Lord, the righteous Judge, will give me on the day of his return.[14]

- Let us not neglect our meeting together, as some people do, but encourage one another, especially now that the day of his return is drawing near.[15]

- Dear brothers and sisters, be patient as you wait for the Lord's return.[16]

- Now we live with great expectation, and we have a priceless inheritance—an inheritance that is kept in heaven for you, pure and undefiled, beyond the reach of change and decay. And through your faith, God is protecting you by his power until you receive this salvation, which is ready to be revealed on the last day for all to see...So when your faith remains strong through many trials, it will bring you much praise and glory and honor on the day when Jesus Christ is revealed to the whole world.[17]

- Dear children, remain in fellowship with Christ so that when he returns, you will be full of courage and not shrink back from him in shame.[18]

So as much as I hate to admit it, that church sign contains an accurate message. We Christians are supposed to be a bit cross-eyed—looking back at the cross while at the same time looking forward to Christ's return.

Equating Eternity with Christ's Return

As we look to the future for the return of Christ, Scripture builds our anticipation for eternity. Technically, everyone—Christian and non-Christian—has an eternal soul. So eternity is not just reserved for those who believe in Christ. The real issue is whether you will spend your post-death eternity with Christ or apart from him. But the New Testament references to "eternity" seem to equate the term to the everlasting existence that believers will enjoy with Christ after their mortal death. In other words, "eternity" is used in the sense of spending everlasting life with Christ in the new creation that God will establish.

Many of us made a decision to accept Christ as a personal Savior with this understanding of eternity. And why not? Jesus himself encouraged his followers by assuring them that they would be with him in heaven.

> Don't let your hearts be troubled. Trust in God, and trust also in me. There is more than enough room in my Father's home. If this were not so, would I have told you that I am going to prepare a place for you? When everything is ready, I will come and get you, so that you will always be with me where I am.[19]

And the writers of the epistles were equally descriptive in their references to our eternal life.

> That is what the Scriptures mean when they say, "No eye has seen, no ear has heard, and no mind has imagined what God has prepared from those who love him."[20]

> Dear friends, we are already God's children, but he has not yet shown us what we will be like when Christ appears. But we do know that we will be like him, for we will see him as he really is.[21]

And the apostle John, before describing his vision of the holy city's gates of pearls and streets of gold, made sure that we understood our existence in this enviable place has eternal permanence: "He will wipe every tear from their eyes, and there will be no more death or sorrow or crying or pain. All these things are gone forever."[22]

This aspect of a blessed eternity with Christ is the hope of our faith. It is what enabled those first-century Christians to endure torture. It is what causes twenty-first century Christians in parts of Africa, the Middle East, and Asia to proclaim allegiance to Christ at the consequence of martyrdom. And the rest of us who aren't at risk of being killed for our beliefs nonetheless endure hardships, disappointments, and struggles, yet we maintain spiritual stability knowing that these troubles are fleeting. Our perspective is an eternal one; we are not mired in the circumstances of the moment, because we have an eternal time line in mind. So when the world is crumbling around you and your unbelieving friends wonder how you avoid despair, you can answer their questions by explaining the reason for the hope that is in you.[23]

Eternity Is Here

Maybe my perspective would be different if my life had been harder. Don't get me wrong. I'm very grateful that I had a privileged upbringing in the comforts of the Western world. I never really experienced persecution for my Christian faith (except on a few occasions when friends from elementary school came to my house to play and made fun of the missionary map in my room). If my life would have had more difficulty, the prospects of a future life in heaven might have been more essential in my life. But the appeal of heaven wanes in direct proportion to the ease of my life. Maybe the same is true for you. When life is relatively easy and enjoyable, heaven doesn't seem like such a big deal.

The presentation of Christianity that I received in my younger years placed too much emphasis on going to heaven. For me, that had no immediate attraction. I knew it would be important in the far distant future, but it seemed to have little relevance in the here and now. Tragically, the emphasis on heaven overshadowed equally important aspects of salvation (all of which would have been more immediately relevant to me). Almost lost in the shine of the promise of the pearly gates and streets of gold were the spiritual principles of other aspects of salvation. These other components could have drawn me closer to God if I had focused on them. I knew them intellectually, but they never became the focus of my appreciation of salvation.

Forgiveness of Sins

> You were dead because of your sins and because your sinful nature was not yet cut away. Then God made you alive with Christ, for he forgave all our sins. He canceled the record of the charges against us and took it away by nailing it to the cross.[24]

Oh sure, I had been told that Jesus died on the cross to forgive my sins. But that wasn't really presented as the carrot on the stick to lead me to Christianity. The ultimate reward that was dangled in front of me was heaven. The death of Christ on the cross—the price he paid to achieve God's forgiveness of my sins—was minimized, and the prospect of heaven was maximized. As a result, I took the entire aspect of the saving work of Christ on the cross for granted. I knew I shouldn't sin, but it didn't seem to be any big deal if I did. I was clueless about the consequences of continually sinning. All I cared about was the fact that it didn't invalidate my "get to heaven free" ticket.

A New Nature

> This means that anyone who belongs to Christ has become a new person. The old life is gone; a new life has begun.[25]

Here is a clue that eternity begins at salvation and isn't postponed until we get to heaven. We have a new life that begins at the moment of our salvation. A story of salvation that oversells heaven and undersells our new nature retards our spiritual growth. Progress in our Christian life is jeopardized because we don't realize that the old nature is actually dead and that a new paradigm for spiritual living has taken effect.

The Indwelling Presence of the Holy Spirit

> And now you Gentiles have also heard the truth, the Good News that God saves you. And when you believed in Christ, he identified you as his own by giving you the Holy Spirit, whom he promised long ago. The Spirit is God's guarantee that he will give us the inheritance he promised and that he has purchased us to be his own people. He did this so we would praise and glorify him.[26]

Imagine that! God's guarantee that his salvation is real is his own immediate presence in our lives. This is no little mini-God sitting on our shoulder and whispering in our ear what is good behavior and what is bad. This is the almighty God of the universe, in the person of the Holy Spirit, indwelling our lives with his presence and power. This was explained to me as I was growing up, but it was downplayed. It took a backseat to the promise of heaven. Maybe my spiritual instructors were afraid I'd turn Charismatic on them. What a shame because I missed the full impact of what the Holy Spirit is all about.

Freedom from the Power and Snare of Sin

> And because you belong to him, the power of the life-giving Spirit has freed you from the power of sin that leads to death.[27]

You can be told at the moment of your salvation that you have a new nature, but the reality of that fact seems questionable the very next time you are tempted. Let's face it. The death of the old nature doesn't seem believable when you're struggling to escape from the grasp of something that is supposed to be dead. So I would have benefited from learning early on in my spiritual life that God had given me the power to overcome the pull of sin.

God's Concern for Social Justice

> This means that anyone who belongs to Christ has become a new person. The old life is gone; a new life has begun![28]

Our salvation transforms us immediately in the sense that we are infused with God's presence. Changing our old ways of thinking may take a while, but we can have God's sensitivity to the extent that we allow it. That means we have the ability to start thinking as God thinks. For many of us, that means being more sensitive to the suffering of others, just as Christ was. Walking right by the homeless with little regard to their condition is far too easy for me. Christ wasn't that way. He stopped and ministered to them. Reading the headlines and skipping the stories about the plight of the poor in India and the AIDS victims in Africa is too easy for me, but Christ was attentive to people like these. He seemed to prefer to be with them much more than he wanted to hang out with the religious types. I wish I had been as concerned about social conditions for the first 37 years of my Christian life as I was about having my ticket to heaven stored safely in the underwear drawer of my mind.

Eternal Life Starts Now

I'm very appreciative of all the people who brought me to a saving knowledge of Jesus Christ and who spent time and energy teaching me spiritual principles. These were people who loved the Lord, and they were genuinely concerned for my salvation and my spiritual growth. They were certainly well-intentioned, but I wonder if they were a bit misguided. I was raised with the notion that heaven is the reward of the Christian life. And when do you get rewards? You get them at the end of the race or the project. And in Christianity, the end is when you die or when

Christ returns, whichever comes first. That is how it seems, but that is not how it is.

I'm looking forward to heaven and the new creation. I'm not quite sure what they will be like, but I'm trusting God that all of it will be good. Great, in fact. But after 37 years of supposing that heaven is the ultimate reward, I've drastically changed my mind. I can see how a cursory reading of Scripture might suggest that is the case, but a closer understanding of Scripture teaches just the opposite. The real reward of our salvation starts immediately when we give our lives to Christ. Heaven is just a nice bonus that usually comes long after eternity commenced.

The reward of our salvation is not eternal life in heaven. Rather, it is a direct and personal relationship with God. And that relationship starts immediately at the moment of our salvation. There is no probationary period. We have immediate and direct fellowship with God from the instant of our salvation. That moment, coincidentally, is also the beginning of our spiritual eternity.

Let's go to the ultimate source on this—Jesus Christ. In his prayer to his heavenly Father shortly before his crucifixion, this is what Christ said about our eternal life:

> Father, the time has come. Glorify your Son, that your Son may glorify you. For you granted him authority over all people that he might give eternal life to all those you have given him. Now this is eternal life: that they may know you, the only true God, and Jesus Christ, whom you have sent.[29]

Did you catch that? Jesus gave the succinct definition of eternal life as knowing God. This concept is simply profound and profoundly simple. Notice that Christ's definition includes nothing about heaven. It should also be recognized that "knowing God" is a present-tense experience. It is here and now. It is not something that is postponed to some unspecified date in the distant future when we hear the flapping of angel wings.

The same sense of immediate possession of eternal life is conveyed in John 3:16 (which isn't surprising because this verse is another one of Christ's explanations on the subject): "For God loved the world so much that he gave his one and only son, so that everyone who believes in him will not perish but have eternal life."

Notice the immediate cause and effect in this verse: When you believe, you have eternal life. The word "have" in John 3:16 is in the present tense. It means "to possess right now." But more than that, it conveys the meaning of continued possession. Jesus was saying that our saving belief in God allows us to immediately possess and keep on possessing eternal life. We have it now and for all of eternity that follows.

Knowing God Is Better than a Ticket to Heaven

Without meaning to minimize heaven in any way, I don't think it is the best-selling feature for salvation. It puts the emphasis on the wrong object and at the wrong time. An emphasis on spending eternity in heaven causes us to focus on a place and circumstances at some speculative time in the future. All of that is wonderful, but it doesn't really materialize into an abundant spiritual life for us right now.

God didn't design salvation simply to give us a place to be enjoyed at some unknown date in the future. The object of our salvation is God himself—knowing him personally. And as we know him better, we will love him more. And a deeper understanding of God will create an abundant life for us. It is an eternal relationship that begins at the moment of our salvation.

Yes, heaven will be nice. But we're missing the best part of eternity—knowing and enjoying God—if we mistakenly think that we have to be in heaven to experience it.

<hr />

When my children were little, my wife and I made the mistake of telling them that we were going to take them to Disneyland in ten months. We thought that the anticipation of the trip would be as much fun for them as the actual event. We were right in theory, but our timetable was off by about nine months, three weeks, and six days. Their attention span was too short and ten months was too long to sustain their interest level. For them, they actually had to be inside the Magic Kingdom before they could get really excited about seeing and touching Mickey Mouse.

There is a spiritual analogy here (although I realize I'm on shaky ground because my metaphor uses Mickey Mouse for God). I'm looking forward to heaven, but I'm not anxious to do what it takes to get there. I'll gladly take it when it comes, but I'm in no hurry. My attention span doesn't allow me to look that far out (and my life isn't all that bad). But here is the great thing about salvation. We don't have to get inside the "Magic Kingdom" to see and touch God. He comes to us where we are and as we are.

Seeing God will be much easier when we realize that we don't have to be looking for him in the heavens at some far distant future date. We need to change our concept of what eternity is all about. It's not about setting up residence in a celestial place. Rather, it is building a relationship with a divine Being. It is not something that happens in the future. It is happening right now for those of us who are disciples of Christ.

God will be much easier to see if we stop staring at heaven and start looking directly at him.

Getting a Glimpse of God

BEING LIKE YOU WERE WHEN YOU ACCEPTED CHRIST

King Solomon must have known a few things about marriage because he had 700 wives.[30] We might ordinarily be suspect of the advice from any guy who married that often, but we can trust Solomon's writings in Proverbs because these instructions were divinely inspired (literally, "God-breathed") for our benefit.[31]

Knowing that passion can cool over time, Solomon instructed his son to recommit to his wife with the same enthusiasm and delight that characterized their early years of romance (but Solomon was much wiser than I am, so he said it in fewer words than I have used): "Rejoice in the wife of your youth."[32]

Solomon was encouraging his son to remember those things that first attracted him to his wife. If he would focus on those characteristics that he first found appealing, his love for his wife would be rekindled. This is a sound principle that transcends the marriage relationship. The apostle Paul suggested that we use a similar technique for reviving our love for God.

⌒

The apostle Paul considered the Christians in the church at Colosse to be strong in their faith. In the following passage from his letter to them, he compliments them on their spiritual commitment, but then he immediately gives them advice for maintaining that commitment:

> Though I am far away from you, my heart is with you. And I rejoice that you are living as you should and that your faith in Christ is strong. And now, just as you accepted Christ Jesus as your Lord, you must continue to follow him. Let your roots grow down into him, and let your lives be built on him. Then your faith will grow strong in the truth you were taught, and you will overflow with thankfulness.[33]

If Paul has this instruction for people who are already strong in their faith, we ought to pay attention to what he says because it is apparently applicable wherever we are in our spiritual journey.

Just As You Accepted Christ

Just as Solomon encouraged his son to recommit to loving his wife as he had when they were first married, Paul instructs mature Christians to follow Christ "just as you accepted Christ Jesus as your Lord." In other words, he wants us to remember those aspects of Christ's character (and our condition) that motivated us to accept Christ as our Savior.

The attributes of God are immutable and everlasting, but they may appeal to us in different ways depending upon our personal circumstances. Some of us may be drawn to his love; others of us may be attracted to his forgiveness. Someone may be impressed with his mercy, and another person might have an overwhelming sense of his holiness. What impressed you about God at the time of your salvation? Paul says to reflect once again on that attribute of God.

Conversely, we all come to God with our own unique set of circumstances and feelings. In other words, we've got baggage that we need to dump at the base of the cross. Some come to Christ with a sense of guilt and shame; others come with relief and enthusiasm. Some come crying for rescue; others are crying for forgiveness. Regardless of our personal situations, if our acceptance of Christ as Savior is sincere, we all approach him in humility and submission. The sum and substance of these emotions and attitudes are what Paul says we should rekindle in our hearts.

Continue to Live in Obedience

The essence of accepting Christ as Savior is our commitment to follow him. We committed ourselves to be his disciples—Christ followers in the truest sense. At the moment of our salvation, we were resolved in our pledge of obedience to his will and principles.

Over time, we commonly waver in our obedience. We let sin slip into our lives. We tolerate things that displease God. We become indifferent to aspects of our behavior that God views as inappropriate for his followers. Paul says we should bring a halt to such behavior and recommit ourselves to the same degree of obedience that we pledged at the moment of our salvation.

Grow in Faith

What is the result of returning to God just as we accepted Christ Jesus as our Lord? Does this mean to repeat a ritual, always going back to the place of beginning to start again on the right path? Absolutely not. Paul indicates that our recommitment to love Christ just as we did when we first accepted him will actually move us further along in our love for God. Our spiritual roots will grow deeper in him, allowing us to get richer nourishment than we previously obtained. We might have been strong in our faith before, but returning to Christ and loving him as we did at the start will make us even stronger in our faith. We'll have deeper insights about him, and our understanding of his truth will be even more compelling to us.

Returning to God with the same intensity that we had when we first accepted him as Savior will strengthen our relationship with him. Our love for him will intensify. We'll come to a better understanding that eternal life is not about the quantity of life, but about the quality of our life lived in fellowship with him.

⌒

Over time, our concern for self and the worries of life can obscure our vision of God. If that happens, we should look to God in the same way we did when we first accepted Jesus Christ as our Lord and Savior.

...Because My Christianity Is Incognito

Not long ago, I joined a gym. Over the years I've been sporadic in my commitment to the muscular arts, but the necessity to resume an exercise program recently became obvious to me on several levels (primarily the level around my belt). The workout area at my gym is divided into three main sections, two of which I never use. There is the cardio section filled with treadmills, elliptical trainers, and stair climbers. I ignore this section because if I'm going to move my legs that fast for that long, I want to travel. The gym also has a large aerobics room. Although I've never been in this room, I know what goes on in there because it has a glass wall that invites a view of the participants, who do things with mats or inflated orbs. Their activities seem a little feminine, but that's not why I avoid them. I chose not to participate because the activities look difficult and stretchy.

I spend all of my time at the gym in the largest section—the one dedicated to weight lifting. This section is so large that it is divided into three subsections that are easily distinguishable by the degree of difficulty.

The low end of the ability scale has machines with thickly padded benches covered in purple vinyl (the color is a dead give-away that these machines are for the beginners). Each machine has a large stack of weight plates (usually five pounds each). You select the weight for your exercise on each machine by inserting a key at the desired depth of the weight stack.

The machines in the next level don't have stacks of weights as part of the assembly. You have to add the weight yourself. These weights come in discs of varying sizes, ranging from five pounds to fifty pounds. (Imagine my embarrassment when I have to ask a woman and a small boy for help placing the 50-pound discs on my machine.) The benches on these machines are covered in red vinyl, but they have no padding (a clue that this section is tougher than the purple section).

The most advanced section has the free weights. No machines here. Just barbells, more and bigger weight discs, hand weights, and curl bars. You can easily tell from a distance that this section is hard-core because the wood benches have no vinyl covering.

The people who work out in the weightlifting section observe a strict social stratum. It is an unspoken code of behavior, but it is quickly and painfully obvious when the uninitiated violate the social protocol. Basically, you shouldn't venture beyond the boundaries of the section reserved for your abilities.

Much to my chagrin and humiliation, I violated the protocol. Not at first, because I started in the purple section (where every-one could tell I belonged). But I had past experience with such machines, so I eventually made occasional visits to the red sec-tion, where the other weight lifters tolerated my presence. But alas, my fatal mistake was to presume that I could enter into the sacrosanct free-weight section. No one told me I was prohibited from the free-weight section (that would have required someone in that section speaking to me, which never happened, ever). And no one in the free-weight section was ever outright rude to me (although I don't think spotters are supposed to push the barbell down toward my throat when I'm attempting a bench press). But I could tell from the intentional indifference that my presence in the free-weight section was not appreciated. Succumbing to social pressure, I retreated from the free-weight section. And my embarrassment even kept me out of the adjoining red section. I have since then and forever taken solace in the purple section, where the arthritic grandmas and I work out in peace.

The weight lifters' code of behavior was a curious thing. I paid the same gym fees as the other guys (and a few women) in the free-weight section. I knew the etiquette for using barbells, and I was as unobtrusive as possible. I even dressed like the other guys in the free-weight section (except my T-shirts have sleeves, which prompted one grandma in the purple section to say, "At least you aren't trying to show off muscles you don't have"). I had every right to be in the free-weight section, but I was made to feel like an outsider—unwanted and out of place. As a result, I retreated, and my workout regime has suffered as a result.

This situation bears a striking similarity to my life as a Christian in a secular society. I feel like I'm a weakling being ostracized from the free-weight section of our culture. Some outspoken people in the arts, politics, professions, government, and education don't really want me—an evangelical Christian—living, working, and contributing in their world. They can't kick me out, but they can make me feel uncomfortable. So occasionally I'm tempted to retreat to the purple section of life, where I can live out my faith in relative obscurity. But to do so would jeopardize my development and growth as a Christian. I would bury myself so far from the culture that I would barely be able to see God from where I was hiding.

As late as the 1950s, people looked to Christians to set the standard for socially acceptable behavior. For the most part, Christians were known for a brand of morality that included abstaining from smoking, drinking, swearing, and illicit sex. Non-Christians didn't necessarily consider such conduct to be sins, but most people believed that the behavior of Christians was good, right, and true. (Just look at those old *Leave It to Beaver* episodes. The Cleavers wouldn't be classified as committed Christians, but their behavior was Christianesque.) During this time, Christians didn't have to worry so much about explaining the doctrines and principles of their faith. Instead, Christians' spirituality was defined for the benefit of secular society by the Christians' external behavior.

Interestingly, Jesus preached against religion that is defined by external conduct. He embraced sinners, such as prostitutes and tax collectors, but he was critical of the Pharisees and Sadducees, who were religious on the outside but callous toward God in their hearts. Christ called them "whitewashed tombs—beautiful on the outside but filled on the inside with dead people's bones and all sorts of impurity."[1] That should be a clue for us as to how he feels about a faith that is defined by external conduct.

But in the 1960s, our society began a huge cultural shift toward the worldview of moral relativism—a philosophy that considers propositions about reality as neither simply true nor false. Instead, our culture considers that our beliefs are in transition and depend on the social and linguistic contexts of each particular situation. In other words, truth is relative. What's true for one person may not be true for another. What's true in one location may not be true somewhere else. And what's true today may not be true tomorrow. Thus, we no longer have a generally accepted code of conduct. In particular, people reject Christian morality because it is based on the now-offensive proposition that God has clearly delineated standards for what behavior is correct and what behavior constitutes sin. Unlike churchgoers in the 1950s, Christians of the twenty-first century can no longer let our behavior define our faith because our conduct and the attitudes that prompt our conduct are viewed as antiquated, narrow-minded, and judgmental.

Within one generation, Christians have gone from being admired by the culture to being marginalized. We were once emulated, but now we are tolerated and sometimes derided. Vocal critics of our faith condemn us as being out of touch and out of place. Some of the criticism is deserved. Sensing that they are increasingly at odds with the culture, *some* Christians seem to have responded in one of three ways:

Become Invisible

Rather than stand out and be ridiculed, many Christians have opted to be absorbed by the culture. For some of them, this was just the lesser of two evils—compromising was easier than standing against the overwhelming tide of cultural opposition. For other Christians, the transition was easy because they were more interested in the attractions of the world than carrying the cross of Christ. Either way, the Christians who have opted to blend in have forfeited their distinctiveness as Christians. As far as their faith is concerned, they are invisible. They no longer have any leverage with which to be salt or light to the world around them.[2] Instead of being able to persuade the culture, they are imitating it. Instead of engaging the culture in dialogue about spiritual matters, they are emulating it. Instead of influencing the culture, they are infatuated by it. Let's face it—it's impossible to have any kind of a positive impact if you are invisible.

Become Isolated

Some Christians refuse to concede and compromise with the culture, but they are also reluctant to buck the trends. So they decide that fleeing is a better option than fighting. As society has become more hostile toward Christianity, these disciples of Christ have chosen to segregate themselves from society. I'm not saying that these Christians have opted for communal living in the desolate hillsides outside Zortman, Montana, far removed from the influences of Hollywood and New York City and the celebrities that populate those cities. No, these Christians are still living in their same houses, but they isolate themselves from secular society by unplugging from their secular contacts and affiliations. They consider separation from the world to be safer and more spiritual than integration with the world, so they only listen to Christian radio, they only read Christian books and magazines, they only visit Christian websites, and they only watch Christian TV. If they need a repairman to fix the plumbing in their house, they turn to a phone directory that is exclusively Christian (which might include a few pagan plumbers who know that the fish sign in a yellow page ad can snag new business from a few unsuspecting Christian homeowners). Basically, these Christians have circled their spiritual wagons in a defensive move to avoid contact with the non-Christian world. They want a safe, Christian-friendly world, so they have to create their own artificial subculture.

Become Insolent

Some stalwart Christians refuse to compromise and decline to hide. Their response is a combination of anger and (re)activism. They are enraged at the world for being so bad (which is ironic because the world is angry at Christians for thinking that we are so good). To vent their rage and to repudiate the world's immorality, these Christians boycott, march, protest, and condemn. Unfortunately, most of their vehemence is directed at behavior. They are quick to proclaim that the Bible condemns such conduct. But we're no longer living in an age when the Bible is universally respected as the authoritative holy text for morality (as might have been the case a century and more ago). So these Christians are demanding adherence to Bible standards from a society that pretty much considers the Bible to be irrelevant to them. The result is a lot of shouting but no budging (from either side).

If we think of society as the audience for our Christian message, we must realize that such responses by Christians have effectively silenced us. Christians who became invisible have an audience, but they have no message. Those who are isolated have retained their message, but they have no audience. And those who have become insolent have offended the audience and are giving the wrong message.

We've Rendered Ourselves Irrelevant

About a decade ago, two marketing hotshots named Jim Taylor and Watts Wacker researched and predicted the cultural shifts and changes that would impact our society in the next millennium.[3] Their analysis was groundbreaking because they categorized the current social, political, and economic splinter groups of society and arranged them according to "media communes." Taylor and Wacker identified these media communes according to the magazine-buying tastes of consumers. Using this approach, they identified seven distinct groups for which attitudes and habits could be predicted with remarkable precision, including these:

- Seven Sisters (women's magazines)
- Real Guys (men's magazines)
- Intelligentsia (highbrow literary magazines)
- Armchair Adventurers (outdoor, travel, and recreational magazines)
- God Talk (Christian magazines)

They called the God Talk group the newest of the media communes. They found it to be the "most tightly bound of all media communes—the one most informed by an us-against-them mentality."

As a Christian, I dislike being defined by my buying habits instead of my character and beliefs. But what is even more troubling from the Taylor and Wacker research is that we Christians have a pronounced and identifiable us-against-them mentality. Having that mentality is bad enough; that it shows is even worse.

Taylor and Wacker aren't the only ones who feel that way about Christians. I frequently have the opportunity to speak to Christian and secular audiences. When the occasion permits, I ask the audience members to shout out words that describe how the public at large perceives Christians. The most common responses I hear are words like these: judgmental, intolerant, hypocritical, and condescending. These responses are not just from the secular audiences. The Christian crowds use those same words to describe their own public image.

Tragically, Christians have become the twenty-first-century Pharisees. We aren't Pharisees in the sense that we adhere to religious formalities while being hard-hearted toward God in our spirit; most of us Christians are genuinely interested in having the love of God active and pervasive in our lives. But we've done a miserable job of projecting that attitude in the secular arenas. Instead of being identified by the love of Christ, we're known for being cold-hearted, unaccepting, and spiritually arrogant. The attitude of our heart is immaterial to people because they can't see it. Their perception of us is based solely on external impressions, and on that basis we appear to be like the hypocritical and sanctimonious Pharisees that Christ condemned.

No wonder we've become irrelevant to society, with hardly any influence in our culture. How could we expect anything else when we've given folks the distinct impression that we want nothing to do with them?

A Biblical Mandate for Cultural Engagement

Any Christian who believes that God wants us isolated from the world because it is, well, worldly, isn't thinking biblically. Our salvation includes a process of transformation from a worldly way of thinking, but it doesn't involve seclusion from the world. The apostle Paul explained the transformation process this way: "Don't copy the behavior and customs of this world, but let God transform you into a new person by changing the way you think."[4]

Our conversion involves a spiritual transformation in the way we think. Our worldview becomes different. The transformation has nothing to do with geographic relocation, nor does it involve physical separation from sinners. God does not beam us up to heaven immediately upon accepting Christ, nor does he want us to barricade ourselves behind church doors until the rapture.

Being a Christian involves rejecting the world's way of thinking while still living in the world. This is at the heart of the "in but not of the world" phrases in John 17. On the night before Jesus' crucifixion, he talked with his heavenly Father and specifically prayed for his disciples (the 11 who were with him in the upper room at the "last supper") and for all disciples who will ever believe in him (which includes those of us who are twenty-first-century Christ followers).[5] Here is the way he envisioned his disciples' relationship with their respective cultures, whether in the first century or the twenty-first:

> I have given them your word and the world has hated them, for they are not of the world any more than I am of the world. My prayer is not that you take them out of the world but that you protect them from the evil one. They are not of the world, even as I am not of it. Sanctify them by the truth; your word is truth. As you sent me into the world, I have sent them into the world.[6]

Christ specifically said that he does *not* want us taken out of the world. More pointedly, he said that he is sending us *into* the world. But he wants us to be living sanctified lives while we are here. Simply stated: Christ envisions infiltration without assimilation—we'll be a vital, redemptive part of the world without getting caught up in its philosophies and lifestyles.

Some Christians argue that Christ's prayer for us to be sanctified necessitates that we pull away from any significant contact with worldly influences (unsaved people). They contend that the very definition of "sanctification" means that we are to be holy (Latin: *sanctus*) and set apart. This argument is correct, but only partially so. "Sanctification" is a great Bible word that dates back to Old Testament times, when it was used in reference to dedicating people, altars, and instruments of the Tabernacle. Very definitely, the definition of sanctification means that something is dedicated to the Lord as holy and set apart, but not in the sense of being placed in a cabinet for protection. The full definition conveys the sense of being dedicated to (set apart for) service or use in some divine manner.

We can easily understand that implements in the tabernacle can be sanctified for use in the worship of God. But we must not lose sight of the fact that God considers us to be sanctified for his use in redeeming the lost members of our society. We need to picture ourselves as agents of the transformation that God intends to accomplish in our culture through our sanctification. To help us understand this concept, God gives us role models in the Old Testament:

- Daniel was selected for an elite governmental training program in pagan Babylon despite his Hebrew heritage because he was "well versed in every branch of learning...gifted with knowledge and good judgment, and... suited to serve in the royal palace."[7] Daniel became instrumental in establishing governmental policies during the period when the Jews were living in captivity.

- Nehemiah was also a Jew, and he earned the favor and respect of the king of Persia and was placed in the highly trusted position of the king's cupbearer.[8] Through his relationship with the king, Nehemiah was able to procure permission and funding for rebuilding the previously destroyed city of Jerusalem.

- Joseph (the owner of the multicolored coat, not the stepfather of Jesus) was found to be capable and creative, so Pharoah elevated Joseph to be second in command over all Egypt. Joseph's administration brought famine relief to everyone in that part of the world, including the entire household of Jacob (Joseph's father), which kept the patriarchal lineage alive.

These individuals managed to infiltrate their cultures with exemplary behavior in ways that gave them influence and credibility. Yet they remained true to their spiritual heritage and did not assimilate the customs of the pagan cultures in which they lived. They are examples for us to follow.

Living Up to the Great Commission

The famous last words of Christ are a pretty good mission statement for Christians:

> Go and make disciples of all the nations, baptizing them in the name of the Father and the Son and the Holy Spirit. Teach these new disciples to obey all the commands I have given you.[9]

These words, known as the Great Commission, are the resurrected Jesus' instructions to his disciples shortly before he ascended to heaven. The instruction is equally applicable to us. This sacred charge by Christ is a fundamental tenet of our faith—to bring the good news of Christ's salvation to others. And we are further charged with discipling those who respond to Christ in their newfound faith.

There is only one place to find people to disciple—in the world. That means that we must venture out into the world, and we can't keep our faith a secret. We can't fulfill the Great Commission if our faith is invisible, or if we don't venture beyond the property boundaries of the church, or if we're hostile to the very people to whom we're supposed to present the love of Christ.

The culture's growing animosity toward Christianity, whether deserved or exaggerated, has caused many Christians to neglect the Great Commission. We're glad to defer this responsibility to a pastor (who we hope can present a compelling message to any unsuspecting reprobate who happens to walk into a church service), but we ourselves are reluctant to be too public about our faith. After all, we don't want to be tarnished with the bad reputation that Christians have obtained. We would rather blend in to the culture and keep our Christianity incognito. But the problem with this approach is that we are ignoring the clear instructions of Christ to have a proactive role and a positive influence in the culture.

If we chose to hide our affiliation with Christ because we're concerned about a cultural backlash from our network of family, friends, and work associates, we will disobey Christ's directive to fulfill the Great Commission. Such outright disobedience is a condition that affects our spiritual vision. We'll continually have difficulty seeing God as long as we're living in denial of our responsibilities to bring Christ to a culture that is in dire need of him.

❦

A friend of mine is a successful businessman in Spartanburg, South Carolina. He is respected in his community for both his business skills and his Christian character. He has successfully managed to infiltrate his culture without being assimilated by it. On a visit to his office, I happened to notice a quote he had framed and hung on the wall behind his desk. It was titled "The Cross to Golgotha" and was written by Scottish soldier and clergyman George MacLeod. It fits my friend's approach to bringing Christ to his community and starts like this: "I simply argue that the cross be raised again at the center of the marketplace as well as on the steeple of the church."[10]

I agree with the sentiments of George MacLeod. We've kept the cross of Christ fastened on the front wall of the sanctuary too long. It is time to raise it again at the center of the marketplace because Jesus didn't spend most of his time in religious settings, and he certainly wasn't crucified in one. Instead, he spent the bulk of his time with the people in the streets, in the marketplaces, and in their homes. And he was crucified alongside a public thoroughfare, where any passerby could see him.

So let's bring the cross of Christ, and what it represents, back to the center of public discourse. Instead of hiring Christian lobbyists, let's place Christians into politics and the highest places of government. Instead of boycotting movies, let's inspire a new generation of filmmakers who will deal with spiritual themes of forgiveness and redemption. Instead of just protesting at abortion clinics, we should have more Christian health care professionals. Homeschooling won't seem like our last resort if we have more Christians in education, in the classroom, and on the school boards. And instead of protesting the National Endowment of Arts, we need to produce more artists with a Christian worldview. We can accomplish all of this as we plant the cross of Christ firmly in the center of our cul-de-sacs.

But as we do so, we need to understand the culture and be prepared to give a compassionate, articulate, and rational explanation for our Christian worldview. We shouldn't try to force society to change its behaviors. Instead, we cooperate with God as he transforms the way people think so they can understand that Christ is the answer for every human need. Once they are connected with Christ, the Holy Spirit can work on changing how they think about their conduct.

The Bible mandates that we bring Christ to the people with whom we live and work in a way that they will understand and find relevant to their lives. We must reach them on their level, just as Christ came to our level to save us. And in the process of helping others to see Christ, our own view of him will improve.

HAVING A READY EXPLANATION

I must confess to sometimes having a few doubts about my faith. Not usually doubts about whether it is true—I'm pretty solid there. My doubts usually circle around the issue of whether other people can reasonably believe Christianity. With all the cynicism that exists, is anyone really going to take the time to give Christianity an objective, considered, dispassionate analysis?

In moments like these, when I reflect on the rational foundations of my faith that I wish other people would consider, I see God more clearly. This is ironic, or maybe it isn't. The presentation that I rehearse in my mind to give to an unbelieving friend has the effect of persuading me once again that Christianity makes sense.

$\backsim$

Some Christians are particularly gifted and comfortable with "sidewalk evangelism." They walk up to strangers and try to initiate a conversation about becoming a Christian. I'm not one of them. I never have been—especially when my youth pastor forced a bunch of us high school church kids into doing so at the mall. It seemed so awkward and wrong for me, so I decided that such testimonial ambush tactics were not going to be in my religious repertoire. Yes, I knew the Great Commission commanded me to make disciples in Jerusalem, Judea, and the uttermost parts of the world, and my youth pastor said that the neighborhood shopping mall constituted my Jerusalem, so that left me staring down the barrel of the canon of biblical authority if I refused. I admired my fellow Christian teenagers who could pull it off, but it wasn't for me.

I've been feeling halfway guilty for more than two decades about this. But I've recently come to the conclusion that a confrontational witnessing technique probably isn't for many Christians, and that's okay. In fact, it may not be the preferred method for most of us. It might have been for the apostle Paul, but perhaps it wasn't for Peter (who messed up his chances as he was standing around the fire pit at the court-yard when Jesus was under arrest). Regardless of whether he was bad at it, Peter gave the rest of us instructions that I can live with: "Always be prepared to give an answer to every-one who asks you to give the reason for the hope that you have. But do this with gentleness and respect."[11]

This verse contains several important directives. First (and foremost for me), it removes the "surprise attack" strategy from evangelistic endeavors. In other words, I don't have to approach strangers. Peter doesn't tell us to have a good catchy opening line. ("If you died tonight, are you confident that you'd be in heaven tomorrow morning?") And we don't have to use the pretense of taking a "religious survey." All we have to do is have an answer. That presupposes that someone else is going to initiate the conversation with a question.

The subtext to Peter's instruction is that Christians live with hope in their lives that non-Christians are missing in theirs. In the first century, hope wasn't considered a virtue. Just the opposite. Hope was sheer and complete foolishness. Nobody in his or her right mind would have hope because life was so bleak, especially if you were a Christian with the destiny of being lion fodder at the next Coliseum event. But those first-century Christians were hopeful (not at the prospects of this life but about the life that would follow their execution).

Twenty centuries later, hope is more highly regarded. People have hope for their children's future, for better health, and for their lottery tickets. But we Christians are the only ones who have a hope that allows us to live in difficult circumstances with a peace that surpasses human understanding.[12] Peter's directive begs the question, why would anyone ask us to explain the hope we have? The answer is simply this: They see a quality of hope in us that brings stability and assurance to our lives that they don't have in theirs. Simply put, other people see Christ in our lives because of the way we live. And though we might not be obligated to approach strangers on the street, we can expect that the hope that faith generates in our lives will be a topic of conversation with those who know us. We should be living in such a way that our Christianity is visible and relevant to others. If we accurately project Christ in our culture, people will be attracted to our faith because of the qualities that it brings to our lives.

Giving a reason for the hope that is in you means more than just putting the gospel message into contemporary words. We need to be ready to apply the message of Christ to the circumstances of everyday life. If we can't show our neighbors and work associates that the gospel is relevant to their lives, we can't blame them for not being interested in it.

Furthermore, Peter wants our response to be couched in gentleness and respect. We must not berate others because their worldview is different from ours. We should begin by acknowledging their point of view (and their prerogative to hold it). And we must be knowledgeable about their beliefs as well as our own so we can explain the distinctions of Christianity (both evidentiary and experientially) that draw us to it.

With our culture steeped in the predominant philosophies of naturalism ("There is no God") and religious pluralism ("All religions are the same"), we need to be prepared to explain why Christianity makes sense to us. We already know that these philosophies might be obstacles to someone embracing Christianity, so we should be prepared to address them. As Paul said, "We destroy every proud obstacle that keeps people from knowing God. We capture their rebellious thoughts and teach them to obey Christ."[13]

Following the witnessing approach that Peter suggests will require that we do our homework. Most of us will need to engage in intentional study of what we believe and why. But we'll be relieved of evangelizing with guerrilla warfare tactics. Many of us, including an unsuspecting public, will appreciate that.

~

I'm sure that Peter's charge to be prepared with a rational explanation of our faith was intended for evangelistic purposes—explaining our faith to someone who doesn't get it yet. And I've used it for that explicit purpose. But the ancillary benefit is that I'm reminded again of why I believe. These become times of recommitment that free me of influences from my upbringing, traditions, and Christian social pressure. The empirical evidence of what the Word reveals renews my trust that what I have experienced is true. In my heart I never doubted God, but this mental exercise certainly improves my vision of him.

...Because I'm Hung Up on Finding His Will for My Life

Few things sound more spiritually noble than wanting to know God's will for your life. Well, actually doing God's will instead of just knowing it probably ranks higher on the spirituality chart, but it all starts with finding his will in the first place, right?

I've spent a great deal of my life in search of God's will. I've devoted time, energy, and prayer to the process. Probably too much of all three, because if I'm honest about it, much of my effort was self-serving. Oh sure, searching for God's will can look like an act of worship, but if we're honest with ourselves, we might discover that we're relying on religious jargon to mask a selfish motivation.

Without a doubt, our search includes a submissive aspect. We genuinely want to know and do God's will because we desire to honor him with our obedience. But our motivation might be disproportionately based on the desire to have a good life. We're aware that God knows and wants what is best for us, so we figure we've got the best shot at success if we follow his plan A rather than screwing up our lives with some plan B of our own choosing.

Some of us have become so obsessed with finding God's will that we've overlooked God in the process. We care more about knowing the design of a divinely planned life than we care about knowing the divine Designer of the life plan. When we get our priorities out of alignment in this manner, knowing God better actually becomes secondary to our search for knowing what he has in store for us.

Maybe we've taken this whole thing about God's will further than he intended.

God isn't hiding from us. He hasn't established residency on some undiscovered planet in a far corner of the universe where his existence is obscured from our view. He is not like the Wizard of Oz, ensconced in a castle of the Emerald City and secluded from view behind a velvet curtain. No, our God has gone to great lengths to make his presence apparent and obvious even to people who are inclined to doubt his existence.

> For ever since the world was created, people have seen the earth and sky. Through everything God made, they can clearly see his invisible qualities—his eternal power and divine nature. So they have no excuse for not knowing God.[1]

Constructing the earth in a way that points directly to God is his mild-mannered way of making his presence known. He's actually much more obvious than that. He has promised to reveal himself to anyone who looks honestly for him: "'If you look for me wholeheartedly, you will find me. I will be found by you,' says the LORD."[2]

And so it is with his will. He isn't hiding that either. Many biblical references plainly indicate that he wants to reveal his will to us and that we should desire to know it. "Teach me to do your will, for you are my God." "Don't act thoughtlessly, but understand what the Lord wants you to do." "We ask God to give you complete knowledge of his will and to give you all spiritual wisdom and understanding."[3]

All of that seems like the perfect setup, right? He has a will for us, he wants us to find out what it is, and he will reveal it to us. It's a spiritual trifecta. So if all of that is true (and we know that it is), why is God's will so difficult to pin down?

You've Got to Know What You're Looking For

When we think about God's will—that elusive plan A that we're so intent on finding—we usually have some specific things in mind. These are usually lifestyle choices that we cast in terms of God's will: What college does God want me to attend? What does he want me to major in?

As we venture past college and wonder about his will for our career, we venture into new queries: Which company should I work for? Should I look for a different job? Should I change careers?

And of course, we've got the ever-popular, relationship categories of personal self-interest: Whom should I date? Should I marry, and if so, whom? What about kids? How many? At what intervals?

We include geography in our investigation of God's will: Where should I live? Should I move closer to or farther away from my family? Does God want me commuting so far when I could be making better use of the time by reading my Bible (or sleeping)?

And we have financial inquiries: Should I move from my current job to a new one that offers a higher salary? Does God want me to buy a new car? A bigger house? Do I have to tithe on the inheritance I received from dead Aunt Kimberly?

If God knows the numbers of hairs on our heads, he certainly is not oblivious to any detail of our lives that is important to us.[4] But questions such as these might not rise to the level in which

God has an opinion one way or the other. In other words, we might be asking the wrong questions because we don't understand what God's will is all about.

It's More About Character than Choices

Many of our personal life quandaries don't have anything to do with God's will. We aren't likely to sense a strong conviction from him about whether he prefers the green blouse or the blue one for today's wardrobe. And he probably won't make his predilection known for boxers or briefs. Likewise, our choice between an Accord or a Camry is just that—our choice. Questions such as these involve what you do. God's will is more about who you are.

It's More About Attitude than Answers

Life will often present you with lots of options, and any of them might be acceptable to God. He isn't as interested in the option you choose as he is in the reason why you chose it. So he's not as concerned about the type of financial investment you make as he is about why you are making the investment. Was it motivated by spiritual stewardship or greed? Did you make the investment to achieve financial independence or in a spirit of acknowledging God's ownership of all your resources? In this context, what you do is not nearly as important as why you do it.

It's More About Relationship than Results

In our quest to know God's will, we're often searching for specific answers for problems that plague us. Is God going to heal me? Is God going to fix my marriage? How am I going to get out of debt? What we often fail to realize is that God's will does not always involve a certain time, a specific course of action, or a particular person. But it is always about the condition of our heart. God's will involves our relationship with him during times of duress more than it centers on the distressing circumstances.

God's Will in Three Parts

We can get a better grasp of God's will if we begin to think beyond the microcosm of our own lives. That's not to say that our daily to-do list is insignificant, but it isn't the only one that God is paying attention to. Let's start with the macro and then focus in on the micro.

At the outset, we need to realize that God has a sovereign plan for the universe. In the meta-narrative that is laid out in Genesis through Revelation, God reveals his will for all of creation. When it was first created, it was good. And then sin came along and tainted it, and under the weight of sin, the earth groans. But when Christ is revealed, the universe will be made perfect. We are participants in that story line, but we don't have the starring roles in the production. We must realize that superimposed over God's will for our individual lives is a much broader, overarching plan for the universe and all its inhabitants.

> Oh, how great are God's riches and wisdom and knowledge! How impossible it is for us to understand his decisions and his ways! For who can know the LORD's thoughts? Who knows enough to give him advice?...For everything comes from him and exists by his power and is intended for his glory. All glory to him forever![5]

In addition to his plan for the universe, God also has a general moral code for humanity. The Old Testament includes a lot of laws. Some of these are moral laws that apply to everyone, but others are civil laws for the people of Israel, and some others are religious laws for the priests of Israel. Making the necessary distinctions to determine the applicability of the Old Testament laws may take more scholarship than we're willing to muster. So most of us can stick with the New Testament for finding the moral behavior that God wants us to abide by. The golden rule from the Sermon on the Mount is easy to understand and readily applicable to everyday life. If you don't want to be cheated, don't cheat anyone else. Similarly, if you don't like being yelled at when you make a slight

driving error, don't flip off a driver who changes lanes and inadver-
tently cuts in front of you. And in case you need something more
black-and-white, the New Testament gets into specific behaviors
that are offensive to God. The Bible refers to such conduct as sin,
but that isn't part of our society's acceptable lexicon. However,
despite the unpopularity of the terminology, the fact remains that
the Bible condemns some behavior as being outside of God's will
for any of us.

> Let there be no sexual immorality, impurity, or greed among you.
> Such sins have no place among God's people. Obscene stories,
> foolish talk, and coarse jokes—these are not for you.[6]

So God has a plan for the universe and a moral code for humanity. And he also has a general will for you (and don't get hurt feelings
over the fact that he has the same general will for all other Christians). The Bible is replete with variations of this theme, but we can
summarize all of them into three overriding components of God's
general will for you.

- God wants you to believe in Jesus and accept him as
  your Savior.

  > The Lord isn't really being slow about his promise to return,
  > as some people think. No, he is being patient for your sake.
  > He does not want anyone to be destroyed, but wants every-
  > one to repent.[7]

- God wants you to be like Jesus.

  > Those who say they live in God should live their lives as
  > Christ did.[8]

- God wants you to know him better and to submit to
  him.

  > We ask God to give you complete knowledge of his will and
  > to give you spiritual wisdom and understanding. Then the way

you live will always honor and please the Lord, and your lives will produce every kind of good fruit. All the while, you will grow as you learn to know God better and better.[9]

This is good news and bad news. The good news is that God's will is much more macro than most of us think. It's all about a relationship with him rather than a specific detail in our lives. That's good news because we don't have to play a guessing game with God. As long as our heart is right with him and we aren't in violation of his moral codes, we have freedom to make choices in the broad latitude he has given to us. But the bad news is that we can't use him like a Magic 8-Ball that gives us an answer to every question. God wants us to decide some things for ourselves.

What God's Will Is Not

With an expanded view of what God's will is, it might be easier for us to understand how our previous concept of God's will missed the mark (and made our search for it so difficult and unfulfilling). Using some metaphors, let's identify what God's will is not.

God's Will Is Not a Tightrope

With an incorrect concept that God's will is all about a specific time, place, event, or person, we run the risk of spending too much time and energy trying to maintain our balance as we walk along the tightrope of what we perceive to be God's will. We think it is a narrow line, and if we lose our balance and take even a tiny misstep, we'll fall and suffer grave spiritual injury. What if you marry a great Christian who is committed to the Lord and is compatible with you in all ways, but this person is not "the one" God has picked for you out of all of humanity? You could fall off the tightrope to your spiritual detriment, and you could start a sequence of mismarriages as someone else marries the person God intended for you, and so on ad infinitum until most everybody is married to the wrong person thanks to the chain of events you started. (And what are the chances that the chain hasn't been messed up already?)

Thankfully, God's will is not like a tightrope. We've got much more latitude than that. To stay with the marriage example, the spousal candidate pool might include many individuals with whom you are emotionally, physically, and spiritually compatible. The important thing is that you stay close to God during the selection process. With that as the foundation—your relationship with God— you might not have to fret about finding the sole individual whom God intends for you because maybe there is a long list of acceptable candidates (and my wife even agrees with me on this).

God's Will Is Not a Maze

If we are constantly playing guessing games with God, we're going to see life as a series of dead ends and wrong turns that necessitate starting over to get back on the right path. For example, if I'm wondering whether it is God's will that I eat an apple fritter for breakfast on the way to work, I can pray that he reveals his will to me by the length of the drive-thru line at Starbucks. If the line extends out of the parking lot, the answer is no, but a short line will be a sign that he sanctions my sugar splurge. In such instances, we aren't really interested in God's will. We're just using him as an excuse to do what we wanted to do all along by stacking the deck of circumstantial scenarios in our favor and calling them signs of God's will.

God's Will Is Not a Bean Under a Cup

Some Christians treat God as if he is like those "hand is quicker than the eye" guys who show you a bean under one of three cups and then rearrange the cups in tornado-like fashion until you are too befuddled to determine which cup is hiding the bean. These Christians often are frustrated in their Christian life because they are needlessly waiting for God to give expressed approval on some decision they are facing. They expect some sign to confirm or reject their proposed action. In essence, they are waiting for God to lift the cup and reveal the bean. They often cite the case of Gideon, who put God to the test with a fleece, making it dry or wet overnight to confirm what God had already instructed Gideon to do.[10] But just because the story of Gideon is in the Bible doesn't mean that God wants us to emulate him in this regard. (Remember, the Bible also contains the story of Judas committing suicide.) Gideon used the fleece experiment with God because Gideon's faith was too weak. (And he acknowledged that he might be ticking God off in the process, so that should be a warning to us.) God has given us a free will, and he is pleased when we exercise it within the very broad parameters of living as Christ lived.

God's will is not about guessing, but it is about guidance. Within the context of God's plan for the universe, his moral code for humanity, and his general will for your life, you have tremendous latitude. On occasion, God may call you to a particular person, place, or activity, and you can rest assured that he'll give you the necessary guidance to get the message if he has one for you. After all, Scripture describes God as our King, our Father, and our Shepherd. Each one of those images conveys the sense of God looking out for our well-being. If he needs to give you a nudge to push you one direction or another, he can and he will. But absent the apparent push by the Holy Spirit, God gives you the freedom to make a decision. Of course, all of this presupposes that you are in close fellowship with God so you can be sensitive to his leading. And that is the point of God's will: It is more about being in close fellowship with him than it is about knowing what's going to happen to you.

A Circle, Not a Dot

The way we view the concept of God's will affects the way we see God. If we believe that his will dictates our every action (with dire consequences if we transgress the narrow and prescribed path), we might view God as a stern father whose primary function is to monitor our behavior to verify our compliance with his mandates. Conversely, if we consider that God's will is simply a matter of suggestions for our consideration, we might mistakenly picture God as an overly permissive father who either doesn't care or believes that consequences don't accompany conduct. We need a correct understanding of God's will to have a correct understanding of God himself.

God's general will for us is that we conform our lives to Christ's nature. Anything we choose to do within that context of imitating Christ can be considered as God's will. To depict this concept graphically, visualize a big circle. Outside the circle are conduct and attitudes that are the antithesis of Christ. Inside the circle is anything that is Christlike. When you are confronted with an issue in life that makes you wonder about God's will, you can perform a quick gut check by assessing whether the choices fall inside or outside the circle. Anything within the circumference of that circle is fine with God.

The task of determining God's will isn't as easy if we mistakenly think that God's will is tied to a particular person, place, time, or event—in other words, if we think we have to pick the right one or we'll miss God's will. With this approach, we've equated God's will to a tiny dot within the circle of God's general will. But the circle actually contains a lot of dots. It's crammed with them. Trying determine which dot is God's will would be an agonizing chore.

If God's will were a dot (which it isn't), God would be rather sadistic (which he isn't). We could be making Christlike decisions but be off by just a little bit—by one or two dots—and then we'd be making the wrong choice. Our stomachs would be in knots as we continually and frantically searched for just the right dots. But God doesn't domineer our lives by sending us on a "God's will" dot hunt.

We have a heavenly Father who wants us to enjoy our relationship with him. He doesn't want us obsessed with searching for his will about the what, where, when, how, and who of our lives. He wants us to be so tight with him that we instinctively think the way he does. When we are at that place, we can relax and make decisions that are consistent with his way of thinking and therefore in his will.

Most of the time, God may have no particular preference whether you choose between being an accountant or a lawyer, settling in Cincinnati or Lexington, or ministering at church as leader of a Bible study group or as a helper in the youth department. The more important issue is whether you are reflecting the love of Christ in whatever circumstance you may choose.

In some instances, God may have a specific calling for *you;* he may want you in a particular place at a particular time so you can be his representative to particular people. The Bible says that Esther was strategically placed in the palace of King Xerxes at a certain time so she could convince the king to spare the Hebrews in the empire from mass annihilation.[11] So too, God might have a specific assignment for you "for just such a time as this." But you don't need to worry about whether this is one of the general decisions in which you have total freedom of choice or whether this is a special assignment choice. Either way, God doesn't leave you hanging.

God gives us great freedom in this process, but he doesn't entirely abandon us. The Holy Spirit uses specific methods to continually influence our thinking. God can speak directly to us through his Spirit, through his Word, and through his people. We should be living in eager expectation of hearing him as he speaks to us, and we need to be continually aware that these are the ways he does it. This too is a part of finding God's will for our lives— knowing that God can specifically direct us in the decisions that he puts before us. We are being Christlike when we are always listening for the voice of our heavenly Father.

So we see a blend of spiritual freedom and dependence in the context of godly decision making. We have great freedom of choice when we are living in the circle of a Christlike life, yet even then we can have the confidence that God will intervene with guidance if he has a specific calling for us. Most of the time, we can choose any of the dots in the circle. But if God wants us to pick a particular one, he'll bring it to our attention.

⌒

I've come to have a deeper love and appreciation for God as I've grown in my understanding of his will for my life. In the past I was like a puppy dog, trailing after God and expecting him to leave a trail of dog-biscuit crumbs along whatever path he wanted me to follow. I knew I needed to be submissive to his will, but I mistakenly believed that his will was narrow and restrictive. My concept of following his will actually demeaned my role in the relationship he wanted us to have. I was waiting for him to spoon-feed me the decisions of my life, never expecting to grow up and learn to make substantive life choices on my own.

Thankfully, even though I viewed myself as incapable of making spiritual choices, my heavenly Father never thought of me that way. He is a loving Father who wants me to experience the freedom in Christ that he designed. He wants me to realize the joy of a Christlike life without the constant angst of wondering whether I picked the right dot.

We have a God who wants us to be in a relationship with him, but not as little children begging for instructions on decisions that we can make ourselves. He wants us to experience an adult relationship with him, one in which we enjoy the presence of each other's company. In such a relationship, our focus can be on him more than our present circumstances, knowing that he'll give us guidance so we won't miss a particular calling if one comes along. But the rest of the time, any particular dot in our circle is simply beside the point.

That's the kind of heavenly Father I want—one who puts me at ease rather than one who puts me on edge.

BEING IN THE SAFEST PLACE

When *we* think of God's will, we have an introspective focus—our concern is on what is going on in our lives. When *God* thinks about his will for us, he has a much more spiritual perspective in mind—his concern is on the development of our relationship with him. When we are looking hard to ascertain God's will, we're focused on people, places, events, or timetables. God's view, however, is on the transformation that is taking place within us.

> Let God transform you into a new person by changing the way you think. Then you will learn to know God's will for you, which is good and pleasing and perfect.[12]

The closer we are to God, the less we have to be worried about deciphering his will, because the more we love him, the more we will be like him. And the more we are like him, the more our conduct will be consistent with his will. As we get to that point, we can stop obsessing about finding his will; we can stop looking at our circumstances and shift our focus onto him.

⌒

"The safest place to be is in the center of God's will." That statement has been attributed to Corrie ten Boom (1892–1983). Corrie was a Dutch Christian who helped many Jews escape capture by the Nazis during World War II. Her autobiography, *The Hiding Place* (made into a movie of the same name), describes how her house in the Netherlands was used as a safe house for Jewish refugees trying to escape German-occupied Europe. Eventually, Corrie and her entire family were arrested. Her father died in a concentration camp in the Netherlands. Corrie and her sister were placed in a concentration camp in Germany. Corrie survived the horror and later traveled as a witness for Christ, proclaiming God's presence and provision in the bleakest of circumstances. If anyone knows about the safety of being in God's will, she does.

Only God knows the number of people who have been influenced by Corrie ten Boom's life. Certainly many Jewish lives were spared death in the gas chambers due to the heroic actions she and her family performed. Many others have been directed to Christ through her testimony (by her words, her books, or her movie). One of the most striking portions of her testimony is the spiritual perspective of her sister, Betsie, who died in the German concentration camp. Betsie's perspective on God's will—that he has no problems, only plans—allowed Corrie to realize that she was a small part of what God was trying to accomplish on a grander scale. After all of the dire circumstances, hardship, and abuse that she personally suffered, Corrie was able to see the big picture of God's will. She was able to see God's will from a global perspective rather than from a self-centric viewpoint.

If we are self-centered in our Christian faith, we think of God's will on a proprietary basis. We want to know how God's will fits in *our* lives. We become spiritually myopic. We see only the way God is operating in the circumstances of our private universe. Our perspective of faith is restricted to direct causal connections with ourselves—what we are doing with God's help, and what God is doing in and through each of us. Our concept of God's will is stuck within the perimeters of our own lives.

If we ever expect to have Corrie ten Boom's spiritual perspective and insight, we need to see God's will as transcending far beyond ourselves. Instead of contemplating how God's will fits in our lives, we need to ask how we can fit into God's will for the world beyond the tiny network of people directly connected to us. Let's dare to conceptualize God as the Lord of the grand universe, not just the Lord of our individual lives.

If we view God only through the restricted lens of what we are doing, we are disconnected from what God has been doing throughout history and currently is doing all around the globe. When we change our paradigm so we're playing on his team rather than expecting him to be on ours, we become a part (albeit a small part) of his redemptive plan for all of humanity. We are no longer in simply a "personal relationship with Jesus Christ"; rather, we begin to understand the communal relationship that all Christians share with each other. We begin to realize what God has intended all along—we are part of the body of Christ. Thus, we share in what God is doing through his body to alleviate poverty in places we will never visit; we are involved in the efforts of Christians who fight for social justice in parts of the world where personal freedoms are not enjoyed; we are connected with the love and care that is extended to the homeless and the poor by our brothers and sisters in Christ in war-torn regions of the world; and we are part of the great spiritual revivals that are ablaze in otherwise predominantly pagan cultures.

We'll never properly understand God's will for our lives if we think only about *our* lives. God's will for each of us must be considered in the context of what God is accomplishing in his kingdom. When viewed from that perspective, we become a part of something that is much more than our individual lives could ever be. Getting excited about what God has in store for you is much easier when you realize it is a part of what he has been accomplishing since the beginning of time.

Corrie ten Boom had God in her life. But she viewed him from the perspective of her life being in the center of his will. Rather than looking inward to see him, she looked outward to see him. Then, when she had the global view of him, her place in his plan made sense.

God is much easier to see if we have the full and complete view of him beyond the parameters of our own lives. Yes, we can see him in our lives because he is active in and through us. But that is only a part of what he is doing. The bigger, more complete view of him is possible only if we step back from ourselves and see God at work in the world and throughout history.

...Because I've Lost the Equilibrium of Renewal and Service

Maybe this is a guy thing that never occurs to women, but I often wonder who was the toughest of those early Christians. John the Baptist seems pretty rugged. I think he could wallop on Matthew (because I consider tax collectors to be pansies). And Peter was a commercial fisherman, so I expect he could clobber Bartholomew (or anyone else with a similarly sissy name). Brothers John and James were probably a good fighting tag team because Jesus nicknamed these disciples Sons of Thunder.[1]

Scripture sets up one particularly interesting grudge match that never transpired. It would be between the apostle Paul and James (the author of the epistle that bears his name, believed to be the half brother of Jesus). Ordinarily, a brawl between two theologians wouldn't have much appeal for me, but I can imagine these guys going at it over an exegetical issue that seems to position them as archenemies of each other. I'm referring to the question of whether we are saved solely by God's grace or if our "works" (the things we do on God's behalf) play any role in our salvation.

A cursory reading of the Bible would cause you to believe that Paul and James are on opposing ends of this argument. Paul is very clear about his position.

- Salvation is a gift. "The free gift of God is eternal life through Christ Jesus our Lord."[2]

- We can do nothing to earn our salvation. "Can we boast, then, that we have done anything to be accepted by God? No, because our acquittal is not based on our good deeds. It is based on faith. So we are made right with God through faith and not by obeying the law."[3]

- We can't take credit in any way for our salvation. "When people work, their wages are not a gift, but something they have earned. But people are counted as righteous, not because of their work, but because of their faith in God who forgives sinners."[4]

- Our salvation is not based on any good works that we may do. "God saved you by his grace when you believed. And you can't take credit for this; it is a gift from God. Salvation is not a reward for the good things we have done, so none of us can boast about it."[5]

But look at what James says about the significance of our deeds. In an in-your-face kind of way, he emphasizes that you don't have salvation without good works:

- A faith without deeds doesn't save anyone. "What good is it, my brothers, if a man claims to have faith but has no deeds? Can such a faith save him?"[6]

- Faith is dead without good deeds. "Just as the body is dead without breath, so also faith is dead without good works."[7]

As much as I like to see a good fight, I don't really think Paul and James would go at each other in a WWE SmackDown. They wouldn't scatter teeth, hair, and eyeballs all across the canvas. First of all, these guys are Christians, and they would be concerned that savage violence would be a stumbling block to the people they are trying to encourage. But more to the point, they really don't hold opposing theological views even though their writings might suggest otherwise. Paul and James actually hold similar theological positions on this issue, but their apparent conflict can be blamed on semantics.

When Paul explains how salvation is obtained, he uses words like "works," "deeds," and "actions" in a negative context. In all of his epistles, and particularly in Romans, Paul emphasizes that salvation is a free gift from God. To drive home that point, he says that our own best efforts at good behavior ("works" and "good deeds") amount to nothing and have absolutely no benefit for our salvation because even at our best we fall far below God's standard (which is sinlessness). If anyone had a "good works" résumé, Paul did, and he says flat out that all of his good actions were just garbage. (He actually used a word that means a derivative of manure, but Bible translators have sanitized the expression in consideration of the fragile sensitivities of easily offended churchgoers.)

> We put no confidence in human effort, though I could have confidence in my own effort if anyone could. Indeed, if others have reason for confidence in their own efforts, I have even more!
>
> I was circumcised when I was eight days old. I am a pureblooded citizen of Israel and a member of the tribe of Benjamin—a real Hebrew if there ever was one! I was a member of the Pharisees, who demand the strictest obedience to the Jewish law. I was so zealous that I harshly persecuted the church. And as for righteousness, I obeyed the law without fault.
>
> I once thought these things were valuable, but now I consider them worthless because of what Christ has done. Yes, everything else is worthless when compared with the infinite value of knowing Christ Jesus my Lord. For his sake I have discarded

everything else, counting it all as garbage, so that I could gain Christ and become one with him. I no longer count on my own righteousness through obeying the law; rather, I become righteous through faith in Christ. For God's way of making us right with himself depends on faith.[8]

James, on the other hand, wrote his epistle to challenge Christians who were stuck in a mediocre spiritual existence. They had no passion for Christ, or at least it didn't show in their lives. And that was his point. If they were truly saved, some evidence of their salvation ought to show up in the way they lived. In other words, if they called themselves Christians, they should be doing the kinds of things Christ did. So James used references to good works, deeds, and actions in a positive context as proof that a person is genuinely committed to Christ. In his epistle, the understanding that salvation comes by faith alone is implicit, but James wants to be very explicit that actions are an indicator of whether a person is really saved.

> So you see, faith by itself isn't enough. Unless it produces good deeds, it is dead and useless.
> Now someone may argue, "Some people have faith; others have good deeds." But I say, "How can you show me your faith if you don't have good deeds? I will show you my faith by my good deeds."
> You say you have faith, for you believe that there is one God. Good for you! Even the demons believe this, and they tremble in terror. How foolish! Can't you see that faith without good deeds is useless?[9]

Okay, so Paul and James won't be having a grudge match. But if they did, I'd want to be the cornerman for James. Biblically, I adhere to Paul's position, so intellectually I believe that I can do nothing to earn my salvation. Hey, even with salvation being a free gift, I don't handle it very well sometimes, so I likely would have no success at all if I were required to earn the whole salvation enchilada by my own efforts. So I'm all in favor of the "faith alone" tenant of Christianity. But emotionally (and selfishly), I'm cheering for James because he brings some notoriety to good works and deeds. Paul minimizes them, but James dignifies them. I'm cheering for James because I'm a hard worker for God, and I'd like a little credit for the things that I do. (I know this isn't a very Christian thing to be saying, but I'd rather be honest with you about it because lying to you isn't a very Christian thing to do either.)

$\backsim$

I'm a type A personality. I'm a hard worker in all aspects of my life—as a provider for my family, as a community volunteer, and as a disciple of Christ. I take a degree of pride in working hard and doing a good job. Some people might say that such pride is a sin, but those people are just sluggards and slackers. I eat their kind for breakfast. Yes, I go overboard with this, but I consider my imbalanced preference for hard work to be a virtue.

So imagine my chagrin every time I hear a sermon on the following passage, which underscores the distinctions between time spent in spiritual reflection and time devoted to acts of service:

> As Jesus and the disciples continued on their way to Jerusalem, they came to a certain village where a woman named Martha welcomed him into her home. Her sister, Mary, sat at the Lord's feet, listening to what he taught. But Martha was distracted by the big dinner she was preparing. She came to Jesus and said, "Lord, doesn't it seem unfair to you that my sister just sits there while I do all the work? Tell her to come and help me."
>
> But the Lord said to her, "My dear Martha, you are worried and upset over all these details! There is only one thing worth being concerned about. Mary has discovered it, and it will not be taken away from her."[10]

Here's my problem with most sermons I've heard on this passage: Martha gets a bad rap. Her activity is criticized when compared to the contemplative attitude of Mary. But let's get one thing straight. In my humble (and correct) opinion, the passage is not teaching that devotions are more important than service. Rather, the passage emphasizes the necessity for a balance between spiritual renewal in Christ and external service for his sake.

Martha's Hospitality

We make a huge mistake if we imagine that Martha was a workaholic who was all about the task but oblivious to the Lord. She had more spiritual insight about Jesus than most of her cohorts, including some of the disciples. Oh sure, when Jesus asked his disciples, "Who do people say that the Son of Man is?" Peter garnered a lot of press by declaring Jesus to be the Messiah, the Son of the living God.[11] But Peter didn't have anything on Martha. She made the same declaration, personalizing it as her own belief, before Jesus raised her brother, Lazarus, from the dead: "I have always believed you are the Messiah, the Son of God, the one who has come into the world from God."[12] So let's begin by giving Martha credit for being spiritually astute.

Next, we'd do well to realize that Martha most probably had the spiritual gift of service. Mentioned in the list of spiritual gifts at Romans 12:6-9, service is a supernatural ability and sensitivity that God gives to some believers to perform tasks that accommodate the care and comfort of others. These are often chores and jobs that others prefer not to do or that get overlooked altogether. But the person with the spiritual gift of service notices people's needs and springs into action joyfully. All of us who are Christians should demonstrate our love for others by acts of service, but those with the spiritual gift of serving are just better at it— they see the need before it occurs to the rest of us, they spring into action, and they do it with enthusiasm.

Martha was all about service, and she had a particular subspecialty in hospitality (which Paul tells all of us that we should be eager to practice).[13] Hospitality conveys a willingness to make others feel welcome whether they are visitors in your home, in your church, or in other settings. It is a very practical aspect of service and is essential to making people feel cared for and at ease. Martha's life was branded with hospitality. Scripture seems to indicate that she was the owner of the house and made it available to her brother and sister. Christ and his disciples often stopped at her house for a meal or to spend the night. Situated in the village of Bethany (just a couple of miles outside of Jerusalem), Martha's house was a convenient retreat for Jesus and the guys as they trekked in and out of Jerusalem.

It doesn't necessarily take a spiritual gift of service to be willing to entertain Jesus as a guest in your house, but putting up with those 12 ragtag disciples probably required all the supernatural strength that Martha could squeeze out of her spiritual gift. When she saw that gang of 13 traipsing up the walkway for an unannounced visit, she knew she'd have to scurry to find and prepare enough food for them all. Despite the logistical nightmare of preparing food and arranging accommodations for Jesus and his posse, Martha welcomed him into her home. That is because she was hospitable and had the spiritual gift of service. She was willing and eager to do the work that others would prefer to avoid so that Jesus and the rest could relax and enjoy staying at her home. And Martha's service made Mary's time of worshipping at Christ's feet possible.

Heavenly Minded but No Earthly Good

I was raised in a household where we were always busy for the Lord. One or both of my parents were commonly at church several nights every week for meetings, services, or choir practice. Many early Saturday mornings, my dad and I cleaned the church property in preparation for Sunday services. He wasn't the church's pastor or janitor, but this was something we did as part of our service to the Lord. (Apparently there is a loophole in child-labor laws if the kid is toiling for free on religious, tax-exempt property.)

This was a good learning and character-building experience for me, but over the years I've come to doubt that any of us had the spiritual gift of service. A sign of spiritual gifting is that you perform an activity with enthusiasm and joyfulness as you sense God working in and through you. With my family, we just did the work because as Christians we were supposed to tackle every job heartily, as to the Lord.[14] I even seem to recall a bit of arrogance in the process (which I'll attribute to myself and shield my parents from such aspersions), in which we might have felt that we—the ones doing so much of the work—were perhaps more spiritual than the freeloaders in the congregation who didn't pitch in.

During my conscripted labor at church, I heard the expression "Some people are so heavenly minded that they're no earthy good." Even at my young age I could interpret this saying without an explanation. Heavenly minded people spent all of their time at church spouting theology, and they were no earthly good because they didn't lift a finger to help out with any of the chores around the place.

With this background, maybe you can understand why I grew up disliking Mary. Come on, doesn't she seem like the "heavenly minded and no earthly good" type? Gimme a break. She's sitting at Christ's feet, listening to what he was teaching, while in the other room, Martha is busting her hump trying to scrounge up some grub for the boys. Martha wasn't just slapping together a cheese sandwich for Jesus. The New Living Translation of the Bible specifically says she was preparing a big dinner that required a lot of preparations.[15] So maybe she was feeding more than just Jesus and his merry band of 12 disciples; additional groupies might have been tagging along as well. Whatever the situation, Mary is just sitting there on her holy heinie, letting Martha do all of the work. (Can you tell I've been harboring bitterness toward Mary for decades?)

Mary's Spiritual Sensitivity

And to make matters worse, this episode from Luke 10 isn't the only time that Mary is guilty of such seemingly "holier than thou" shenanigans. A similar incident is reported in John 12 that finds her sitting at Christ's feet (again!) while Martha was on kitchen duty (again!).

> Six days before the Passover, Jesus arrived at Bethany, where Lazarus lived, whom Jesus had raised from the dead. Here a dinner was given in Jesus' honor. Martha served, while Lazarus was among those reclining at the table with him. Then Mary took about a pint of pure nard, an expensive perfume; she poured it on Jesus' feet and wiped his feet with her hair. And the house was filled with the fragrance of the perfume.[16]

I used to look at this passage in John 12 as further proof that Mary was just one of those Christians who loved the warm and fuzzy part of Christianity but stayed away from the grunt work. But I've come to realize that Mary wasn't dodging work; she was truly and sincerely tuned in to Christ—to the point where she was spiritually insightful without even knowing it. She had no clue that Jesus was just a few days away from being crucified, yet she anointed him with perfume, which Jesus interpreted as a symbol for his burial. The disciples, including Mary, probably thought this was a non sequitur (why would he mention his burial when he was only 33 years old and in good health?), so it must have seemed like an odd reference for him to make. But God wanted this event to occur, and Mary was the one who was spiritually sensitive enough to make it happen.

Seeing Mary in this light caused me to reexamine the setting in Luke 10 when Martha complained to Jesus about the unfairness of Martha serving while Mary was sitting at his feet. I find that I've been hypercritical and unjust in my evaluation of Mary. Here again, we find that she is not just hanging with Jesus so she can elude the culinary chores; rather, she is engaged in the activity that is on Christ's agenda. As the passage reveals, Jesus is not just engaged in idle chatter. He is teaching, and Mary is focused on what he is saying with rapt attentiveness.

Martha's Distraction

Without a doubt, Christ was grateful to Martha for all the hospitality she extended to him on his many visits to her home. And with good WWJD? manners, he must have expressed his appreciation to her. But he viewed and valued her as much more than just a short-order cook and B-and-B matron. In her frenetic acts of service and hospitality (as spiritual as those were), he recognized that she was missing the more substantive aspect of his visit. Having a meal was important, but she really needed to spend one-on-one time with him. Christ didn't want her service to him to obliterate the importance of being with him.

So in response to Martha's complaint about the unfairness of Mary's inactivity, Jesus simply and gently embraced Martha. He didn't scold her for being unspiritual. He didn't deride her for paying more attention to the vittles than to his teaching. But he did point out to her that in the process of serving him, she had become distracted from something far more important than the meal. He explained that she had lost the joy of serving him: "My dear Martha, you are worried and upset over all these details! There is only one thing worth being concerned about. Mary has discovered it, and it will not be taken away from her."[17]

Even though she was actively engaged in serving Christ, Martha had gotten to the point where she couldn't see the divine among the details. We don't know when she crossed the tipping point, but it wasn't about serving Christ anymore; it had become more about getting the meal served while the casserole was still warm. It was no longer about the excitement of having Christ in her home; it had turned into resentment of Mary because Martha was desperate for an extra set of hands in the kitchen.

We don't know about Mary's ministries in her community of

Bethany. Maybe she helped feed the poor, or maybe she visited the infirm, or perhaps she befriended orphans and widows. Whatever her ministry activities were, during the episodes of Luke 10 and John 12, she disengaged from those ministries to spend time with the Lord. For her, these were times of spiritual renewal.

That was what Jesus wanted Martha to realize and experience for herself. Without spiritual renewal, our service for the Lord will turn into an annoying distraction, and that's exactly what had happened to Martha.

The Balance of Service and Renewal

I still think Martha gets a bad rap from preachers who want to emphasize the importance of spending reflective moments with God. They tend to suggest that she didn't love Christ as much as Mary did because she was busy around him rather than quiet before him. But Martha appears to have loved Christ with the same fervor and devotion that Mary had. In these scenes, we see Martha simply expressing her love for him in the manner (hospitality) that God had wired her for. Her failing in the Luke 10 passage was not a lack of love, but a loss of priorities. She let her proclivity for service overshadow her need for spiritual recharging. Her spiritual batteries were being drained.

Many of us are like Martha. We love the Lord, and we love to serve him in tangible ways, employing the spiritual gifts he has given to us. We sense God's pleasure in such service, and that motivates us to ratchet up our ministries another notch. But if we aren't careful, the accomplishment of a task becomes our goal, and service to Christ becomes a by-product. The whole thing is then more about us and less about the Lord. We want the project to get done on time, we want it bigger and better than before, and we don't want any snags along the way. The pressure builds, the stress increases, and the joy dissipates. We're doing it all for the glory of God, of course, but these efforts are actually pulling us further away from him.

In these times of ministry overload, Christ is reaching out to us and saying, "My dear child, you are worried and upset over all these details. You need to be concerned about only one thing, and that is connecting with me."

Serving the Lord should never be so intense that we lose the joy of the Lord.

◦——

I've come to appreciate Mary for what she has taught me. I'm not going to abandon my Martha-like orientation to active service, but I have a mental picture of Mary at the feet of Christ that I use as a constant reminder to keep equilibrium in my worship of God. I don't want my involvement in service to get so extreme that I don't experience the spiritual renewal I so desperately need.

I've been convicted by that expression about people being so heavenly minded that they're no earthly good. As it turns out, an honest examination of my life has revealed that many times I've been so earthly minded that I was of no heavenly good. I was so intent on getting a church project started or some ministry revamped that I became a whirlwind of activity, spinning out of control. Sadly, I often lost sight of God in my frenetic activity. If I saw him at all, he was just a blur. How ironic—I've been guilty of ignoring the one I was attempting to serve.

Those of us who suffer from this spiritual malady would benefit from some deprogramming. For too long we've been repeating the mantra that idle hands are the devil's playthings. We who are vigilant Christians keep our hands busy by being up to our elbows in ministry. Unfortunately, we often take too much pride in the accomplishments of our service. So our hands aren't idle, but the work of our hands often becomes our idol. We've lowered God from the place of highest priority in our lives, and we have substituted the ministries we perform for his sake. Those activities consume too much of our time, energy, and resources. As a result we are left emotionally, physically, and spiritually drained. In that condition, we become resentful of the very ministries and people we were once passionate about.

Martha was busy for the Lord, but her busyness turned into bitterness. Jesus challenged her to moderate the intensity of her activity so she could manage to find appropriate times for spiritual renewal. Then her bitterness could be replaced with God's blessings. What Christ wanted for Martha may be the prescription we need to see God more clearly through the hectic haze of our ministry endeavors.

Getting a Glimpse of God

LEARNING THE ART OF SPIRITUAL BREATHING

You can only push so hard for so long in your ministry activities before your spiritual tank will run dry. You have to build time into your schedule for spiritual refueling. Spending 60 minutes in a worship service on Sunday probably won't be enough, although it certainly won't hurt. You need an appropriate proportion of renewal and ministry to stay balanced.

These words may resound with you if you are gung ho about ministry and service opportunities. But they may sound hollow and useless if you have an orientation toward spiritual refection. If that is your modus operandi, you have no problem finding devotional time with the Lord. Yet an entrenched habit of spending "quiet time" with the Lord doesn't ensure a vibrant and healthy Christian existence. Unless you balance your meditative moments with acts of service, your spiritual life will be off kilter. Instead of a life that is too hectic to experience God's presence, your plight will likely be boredom and spiritual lethargy due to stagnation.

A healthy Christian life requires a balance of both: times

of spiritual renewal and times of service. Just as your physical life requires breathing—with a balance between inhaling and exhaling—your spiritual life requires proportionate and synchronized aspects of a devotional life and a life of servanthood.

The human body has an intuitive and instinctive compulsion to breathe. I won't bother to support this thesis with a citation to medical authority. If you doubt it, just stop breathing and wait about a minute until your body is writhing and contorting as you try to suppress the process of inhaling and exhaling.

My appreciation for breathing's irresistible coercion was heightened during my first (and only) white-water kayaking experience. I had previous experience with the much more tranquil sport of open-water kayaking. I enjoyed the pleasurable endorphins from the serenity of the peaceful paddling, but I also felt ready to increase the adrenaline level of this recreational sport. Unfortunately, my spirit of adventure wasn't matched by sufficient skill. I got caught in a current that separated me from my group, and then I capsized. I didn't have the ability to roll my kayak upright, but I thought I could bail out—while upside down underwater. But then I discovered an equipment malfunction that prevented me from doing so.

The process of drowning was surreal. I was totally submerged in the river, yet my body wanted to breathe. I remember convulsing as I tried to suppress the urge to inhale. Finally, against all rational instincts, I succumbed to the overwhelming impulse to breath and inhaled enough river water to fill my lungs. For a brief moment (which played in slow motion in my mind), I actually inhaled and exhaled water in a spastic and apoplectic manner.

Obviously, I've lived to tell the horrid tale of my attempt at aquatic breathing. That experience has taught me two life lessons: First, God designed us for breathing, and second, that process works better with air than with water.

Breathing provides an applicable metaphor for our spiritual life. Our physical bodies process oxygen with the reciprocal actions of inhaling and exhaling. Each action is done in proportion to the corresponding opposite action. If you inhale too deeply, your lungs could blow up; if you exhale too deeply, you could faint. We inhale and exhale with a measured and compatible rhythm.

In his book O_2, my friend Richard Dahlstrom uses the human breathing pattern as a metaphor for our life of faith, but the life source in the process is not oxygen.[18] To have a healthy spiritual life, Richard explains, we must inhale life-giving strength from God (that comes to us through prayer, the study and meditation of Scripture, solitude, and spiritual reflection). Conversely, a reciprocal exhale must occur (which takes the form of service to others, generosity, kindness, and hospitality). Each aspect is absolutely necessary for our spiritual well-being. We put our spiritual health in jeopardy when we have too much of one or too little of the other.

❧

Inhaling is not more important than exhaling, nor is exhaling more essential than inhaling. They must operate in balance. We get that. But why do so many Christians fail to recognize that spiritual renewal and servanthood must also be balanced and exercised proportionately in our spiritual lives in order to sustain a healthy faith?

All of us may have difficulty seeing God from time to time, but the causes of our spiritual myopia may be different.

Some of us have been exhaling too long. We're spiritually exhausted and exasperated, our lives are frayed and frazzled, and we desperately need to deeply inhale a reviving breath of God's regenerative love. We might have to force ourselves to find a place for solitude in our schedules. This might include disconnecting from ministry for a few moments. But we need to do it, just as we need to breathe.

Others of us have stunted our spiritual growth because we've been inhaling too long without ever exhaling. We love to take God's Word into our lives, but we want to keep it there, abhorring the prospects of a public involvement of our private faith. As a result, our faith has become introspective and stilted because it has been cloistered from interaction with the outside world. To heal this condition, we need to begin the process of exhaling God's love to others in practical, tangible ways. Only then will we be capable of inhaling a fresh spirit into our lives to regain the passion that is tragically missing.

I've been very slow to realize that my ability to see God is determined in large part by my ability to breathe God in and out of my life in a balanced and rhythmic manner.

...Because I Don't Like His Other Children Very Much

As a probate lawyer, I've had many opportunities to conduct "reading of the will" ceremonies after the death of wealthy family patriarchs. You've probably seen theatrical portrayals that make this scenario look ridiculously dramatic. But in real life, it's even worse.

Families who are loving, happy, and cordial seldom get together for a reading of the will. The families with one or more greedy relatives in the mix are the ones that require a family gathering because suspicion runs rampant among them. They all want to be in the same room at the same time so they can keep one eye on each other and the other eye on the lawyer, whom everyone distrusts.

I have a distinct memory of one such family meeting. It was held the day after the grandfather's funeral. The decedent was survived by his widow, their three sons (and the three daughters-in-law), and seven grandchildren (ranging in age from 22 to 32). The meeting started late as we waited for the arrival of the predominate black sheep of the family—a spoiled and ungrateful grandson. We were all seated around a large conference table when his highness walked into the room, dripping in arrogance. I'll never forget his opening comment: "You don't have to like me. But you have to love me because we're family."

I think of that kid's comment when I get exasperated with other Christians. I may not like them, but they are part of the Christian family, so I have to love them. Jesus said so.

Sometimes I wonder if Jesus knew what he was talking about. Or maybe he just doesn't know the Christians I know.

Don't get me wrong. My best and closest friends are Christians. I also have friends who are nonbelievers, but my relationship with them does not go as deep because we don't share the bond of a common faith perspective. The Christian worldview is a great foundation for a strong friendship, and it is the basis of my strongest friendships. But I'm just not simpatico with a lot of Christians, and their feelings toward me are mutual. We are nice to each other, we're polite, and we don't hold an ounce of animosity toward each other; we just lack a degree of compatibility to make us anything other than good acquaintances. We're much like Christian colleagues—we're part of the same organization (Christianity), but that connection is our only point of commonality. We continue on in this tangential relationship, and all is well with our individual and separate worlds.

And then along comes Jesus, who messes with my mind and commands me to love these Christians who are on the periphery of my friendship network. Quite frankly, I'm not sure I can pull off loving them. I'm giving it all I've got just to tolerate them.

⌒

The disciples knew that Jesus was big on family ties. They heard him boldly criticize the Jewish religious leaders for failing to honor their parents as required by the Ten Commandments.[1]

So on another occasion, the disciples were probably shocked to hear Jesus downplay family relationships:

> As Jesus was speaking to the crowd, his mother and brothers stood outside, asking to speak to him. Someone told Jesus, "Your mother and your brothers are outside, and they want to speak to you."
>
> Jesus asked, "Who is my mother? Who are my brothers?" Then he pointed to his disciples and said, "Look, these are my mother and brothers. Anyone who does the will of my Father in heaven is my brother and sister and mother."[2]

Was Jesus saying that when we become Christians, we should cut all ties with our biological families and instead only associate with fellow believers? Of course not. That would make Christianity kind of cultish and a little creepy. Rather, this passage lays the groundwork for what the disciples were going to learn about their spiritual family—the kingdom family into which Christians are born at the moment of their salvation.

A Biblical Mandate to Love Our Spiritual Family

Picture this: Jesus is in the upper room with the disciples on the evening before his crucifixion. They had just finished the "last supper." Christ knows that this is the last chance he'll have to speak with them before his death. Time is short, and every "last word" he speaks to them is loaded with great importance. Bible scholars refer to this scene as Christ's "farewell discourse."[3] Jesus laid out the ground rules for how he wanted the emerging family of Christians to relate to each other.

> As soon as Judas left the room, Jesus said, "The time has come for me the Son of Man to enter into his glory...
>
> "Dear children, I will be with you only a little longer. And as I told the Jewish leaders, you will search for me, but you can't come where I am going. So now I am giving you a new commandment: Love each other. Just as I have loved you, you should love each other. Your love for one another will prove to the world that you are my disciples."[4]

At first, the 11 remaining disciples in the upper room may have thought that Jesus was limiting these words to them. But if they did, they eventually figured out that Jesus intended these words to be applicable to all Christians, just as his prayer in the upper room covered all of us. "I am praying not only for these disciples but also for all who will ever believe in me through their message."[5]

Is This Really a *New* Commandment?

The import of Christ's words is clear. He has given us a new commandment that requires us to love each other. But wait a minute. I raise this question with some trepidation because I don't want to nitpick at anything Jesus says, but is this really a *new* commandment? After all, the commandment to love our neighbors dates back to the time of Moses, when he wrote this command of God: "Do not seek revenge or bear a grudge against a fellow Israelite, but love your neighbor as yourself. I am the LORD."[6] And Christ himself had earlier preached the command to love others in his Sermon on the Mount: "You have heard the law that says, 'Love your neighbor' and hate your enemy. But I say, love your enemies!"[7]

Well, you are correct that this isn't a new commandment if you are thinking of "new" in a chronological context. It definitely was not a new commandment in terms of being recently proclaimed for the first time.

A New "Just as I Have Loved You" Kind of Love

But this commandment did carry new meaning. Christ was bringing a different, fresh, and deeper meaning to an old commandment. He modifies the original love commandment by saying we should love each other *just as he loved us.*

With that adverbial phrase, Jesus brings entirely new meaning to the concept of love. Surely the disciples were still clueless when Jesus spoke these words to them. Only after the crucifixion and resurrection would they begin to understand what real love was all about. But let's face it—we're the same way. Our understanding of love is shallow if we consider it outside the context of Christ's example. Our concept may be romantic, it might be caring, and it might be selfless. But our notion of love—absent a Christian worldview—seems trivial when compared to the love that Christ has shown to us. The depth of his love for us is incomprehensible—we cannot even come close to fully grasping the magnitude of love that compelled the almighty Creator of the heavens and earth to humble and degrade himself to take on human form and then to be tortured and crucified for the rebellious sins of his ungrateful and defiant creatures. So after Jesus' crucifixion, we have a deeper understanding of what love could be about. And it is this deeper version of love—this "just as I have loved you" version—that Christ commands us to apply in our relationship with other Christians. Bottom line: It is a new kind of commandment because he was talking about a new kind of love.

A New "Love Each Other" Kind of Love

It's also a new kind of commandment because Jesus had a specific, limited audience in mind as the recipients of this "just as I have loved you" kind of love. Moses taught that we should love our neighbors, and Jesus expanded that to include the world population at large—our neighbors and our enemies. Accordingly, when Jesus was asked for a point of clarification as to who falls into the category of "neighbors," he told the story of the Good Samaritan to explain that everyone is our neighbor, and apparently, especially people who are strangers to us or who are in need.[8]

But in presenting the new commandment for the "just as I have loved you" kind of love, Jesus narrows the focus. This new kind of love is to be exhibited toward other Christians. Notice Christ's explicit and repeated emphasis on how this love should be displayed by the disciples (and us) to "each other."

> So now I am giving you a new commandment: Love *each other.* Just as I have loved you, you should love *each other.* Your love *for one another* will prove to the world that you are my disciples.[9]

Christ didn't revoke the command to love the people of the world. The "love your neighbor as yourself" charge is still valid and continues in full force and effect. It remains equally as important as the commandment to love God with all you heart, all your soul, and all your mind.[10] Thus, we are to continue to be salt and light to the people of the world through the love that we show them.

But the love that is to exist among Christians is different by quality and degree. For all of eternity, the Father, Son, and Holy Spirit have existed in a special love, unity, and oneness. Humanity could not possibly experience or share in this kind of love—until the work of Christ on the cross. With our salvation, we can now enter into this same love relationship as children of God and "joint heirs" with Christ.

> For all who are led by the Spirit of God are children of God. So you have not received a spirit that makes you fearful slaves. Instead, you received God's Spirit when he adopted you as his own children. Now we call him, "Abba, Father." For his Spirit joins with our spirit to affirm that we are God's children. And since we are his children, we are his heirs. In fact, together with Christ we are heirs of God's glory.[11]

As Christians, we have this special union with God through Jesus. But more than that, it extends mutually among us as believers. That is the point Christ was making to the disciples (and to us) when he described a "just as I have loved you" kind of love that he wants us to experience with each other.

We believers share a kinship through Christ that not only benefits us but also promulgates the gospel message. The love and unity that we share with God and with one another set us apart from the rest of the world. We become identifiable as our love for one another proves to the world that we are Christ's disciples. We become distinct, but not in a socially repulsive way. The quality of our love for each other will be an attractive mystery to nonbelievers. It will bring them to Christ.

At least this is what happened in the early centuries of Christianity. One of the earliest Christian theologians, Tertullian (ca. 160–220), the guy who coined the term "Trinity," reported what the pagans said of the Christians: "See, they say, how they love one another…how they are ready even to die for one another." And E.R. Dodds, a nineteenth-century Irish secular scholar and historian, wrote that the genuine love and unity among Christians was "a major cause, perhaps the strongest single cause, of the spread of Christianity."[12]

Christ didn't put an expiration date on this. The attraction to Christianity caused by the love among Christians wasn't limited to the first couple of centuries following his death. We Christians should still be attracting nonbelievers to Christ by the degree of love, commitment, and unity that we share with each other. But we don't seem to have the same impact in our society as those first- and second-century Christians had in theirs. Have we misunderstood and misapplied the nature of the love that Christ explained to the disciples?

Singing Our Way to Misguided Theology

I was an impressionable kid in the 1960s, the decade of love. America had the whole hippie thing going with the ubiquitous "Make Love Not War" slogan, the decline in morality under the banner of "free love," and Woodstock. Christians weren't left on the sidelines of this lovefest. We even had our own love theme song for that era—"We Are One in the Spirit"—with its haunting melody and simple chorus.

As Christian kids, we used to sing this song a lot. It didn't have much of a beat, but it was about the closest thing we had in the 1960s to contemporary Christian music. Our only other alternative was to sing hymns, so we stuck with "We Are One in the Spirit" and "Kum ba Ya." Yep, we were living on the edge.

One line from the song's chorus stated that others will know we are Christians by our love, so it seemed to suggest that this song was rooted in Christ's new commandment of John 13:33-34. That made it seem all the more spiritual when we sang it. But the song didn't quote the verse precisely, and we were singing it in a kind of euphoric ignorance. Although none of us noticed it at the time, "We Are One in the Spirit" might have theologically misdirected my generation of Christians in two ways.

First, no one clearly explained to us that John 13:33-34 was speaking of a deeper, "just as I have loved you" kind of love. So for many of us, the repetitive singing of the song was simply reinforcing a mistaken belief that we Christians were supposed to be exhibiting plain old ordinary love—the "be nice and caring" kind of love. Our song wasn't imploring us to a higher degree of love represented by Christ's sacrificial death on the cross. We were just singing about the same kind of love that the hippies wrote about on their placards when they protested outside the army recruiting offices.

The song may have innocuously enabled our misunderstanding of John 13:35 in another way as well. We were thinking that the love we were singing about was supposed to be extended to the entire world. We were singing about a "love your neighbor" and a "love your enemy" kind of love. What we sang was close to what Christ said, but we omitted a few crucial words. Christ said the world would know we are Christians by our love *for each other.*

If we had added those three essential words, the entire meaning of the song would have been changed, and my singing would have been aligned with the correct interpretation of John 13:35. But for years my singing was a little off musically and a lot off theologically.

The influence of Christians in our culture hasn't received much positive acknowledgment since the 1960s. Maybe any positive influence started to dissipate when we stopped being distinctive and lost our mysterious appeal. We were singing about plain old love, but our song merely blended in with the popular music of the decade that acclaimed secular love. Our concept of love—the way we talked about it and the way we translated it into action—didn't really distinguish us from anyone else. Masses of humanity—Christians and nonbelievers alike—were into the love thing. It was the common currency and the buzzword of the decade. Love references were printed on T-shirts and posters, and it was the theme of most graffiti pontifications. Our melodic Christian protestations of love simply blended in with the culture's mainstream catchphrase.

Maybe in this regard, not much has changed in the Christian community since the 1960s.

What Does "Love Each Other" Look Like?

How can we as Christians reinstitute among ourselves the "just as I have loved you" kind of love that Christ wants us to extend to each other? The answer may be right in front of us. Perhaps all we need to do is to examine the ways in which we put our love into action toward our closest Christian friends. That may enlighten us to God's expectations for how we should respond to everybody in the entire body of Christ, especially those to whom we are presently indifferent.

The shift to actually loving the Christians whom we have been merely tolerating will not be easy. And the changes we need to make won't be the same for all of us. God convicts and guides each of us in unique ways, so our responses must also be unique. But three biblical principles might provide a good starting place for all of us. If we can begin to integrate these principles into our relationships with all Christians, we'll be moving much closer to the kind of love that Christ wants us to experience in his family.

Sincerity and Respect

The apostle Paul often wrote on the subject of interpersonal relationships between Christians. He entreated us to view each other with dignity, recognizing that God loved each of us enough to die for us. In other words, we need to view each other through the eyes of Christ: "Don't just pretend to love others. Really love them...Love each other with genuine affection, and take delight in honoring each other."[13]

Our love for each other must be sincere. It should be free of hypocrisy and pretending. It should be authentic and without any ulterior motive.

This is a different kind of love than the world has come to know. In our society, love is used as barter. People give it on the condition that they will get an equal amount in return. It is a 50-50 kind of love. In contrast, Paul's term for affection comes from a word meaning family love. He calls us to love each other because we are members of one family. As Christians, we are brothers and sisters with each other because we have the same heavenly Father.

Action

In the ancient church, the disciple John was known for his concern for love among the saints. His epistles are almost entirely devoted to the subject. Jerome, a Bible scholar of the late third and early fourth centuries, wrote that in John's elderly years, when he was carried into any assembly of Christians, he would repeat the same greeting: "Little children, love one another." When his attendants finally got tired of the ritual, they asked John, "Master, why do you always say this?" John replied, "It is the Lord's command. If this alone be done, it is enough."[14]

With this as his perspective, it is not surprising that John wrote this instruction in his first epistle: "Dear children, let's not merely say that we love each other; let us show the truth by our actions."[15] And with John, it wasn't just theory. He also gave specific examples: "If someone has enough money to live well and sees a brother or sister in need but shows no compassion—how can God's love be in that person?"[16]

But all of John's teaching on the subject pales in comparison to the ultimate act of love that Christ showed for us, which is the embodiment of the kind of love we should have for other Christians. Christ said it this way to the disciples in the upper room as he reiterated the new commandment to them: "This is my commandment: Love each other in the same way I have loved you. There is no greater love than to lay down one's life for one's friends."[17]

Rarely are any of us required to lay down our life for a Christian brother or sister. But God commands us to that degree of love. So at a minimum, we should be ready and willing to sacrifice some of our time, our energy, and our resources for Christian brothers or sisters who are in need, whether they are close friends or totally unknown to us.

Intimacy

When Christ prayed in the upper room, he stated his desire that we might experience the same unity with each other that he enjoyed with his heavenly Father: "I am praying not only for these disciples but also for all who will ever believe in me through their message. I pray that they will all be one, just as you and I are one—as you are in me, Father, and I am in you."[18]

This degree of unity among Christians involves accountability, vulnerability, and encouragement. This might go against our instincts to keep our fears and failings to ourselves. But God instructs us to be open and authentic with each other. These aspects are essential to our relationships in Christ, who is most likely to use other Christians as his way of ministering to us.

There is no higher level of commitment than to love other Christians with the "just as I have loved you" kind of love. We can think of lots of reasons to make our commitment at a lower level: Maybe we don't have the time, we don't have the energy, we will be neglecting our very best friends, or the ones we are called to love aren't appreciative. But what we would call reasons, God considers as excuses. He commands us to love each other, so he will give us the capacity to do it. It is a matter of obedience.

It's also a matter of spiritual vision. As we develop our capacity to love the members of our spiritual family—really love them as Christ instructed us to—we'll start enjoying harmony, unity, and oneness of spirit with them. Becoming more sensitive in that manner will improve our vision of God because those are the qualities he wants in our relationship with him.

❧

With a better understanding of John 13:34-35, I now enjoy singing "We Are One in the Spirit." The melody hasn't changed. The song is still simplistic and repetitive, but it helps me to envision Christ in the upper room with his disciples. As I sing the lyrics, I picture Jesus explaining what the disciples couldn't then understand but would later comprehend. I've been exactly like them (although they probably didn't take 40 years to get it).

Every time I hear the song, I'm prompted by God to recommit myself to actually loving the members of the Christian family. Not just tolerating them. Not just talking about love or going through halfhearted efforts to give the impression that I care. I'm challenged to make my love the real deal—extending myself far beyond my comfort level. In those moments, when I'm able to come close to the substance of Christ's new commandment, I start to realize just how much God loves *me*. It is the actualization of what Jesus prayed in the upper room:

> O righteous Father, the world doesn't know you, but I do; and these disciples know you sent me. I have revealed you to them, and I will continue to do so. Then your love for me will be in them, and I will be in them.[19]

God is so much easier to see when you sense his presence in you.

LOVING YOUR CHURCH FAMILY

Those of us who are introverts by nature don't really mind going to church under a figurative cloak of anonymity. We're content to walk into the sanctuary unnoticed, plop down into a seat, sing a few songs, listen to the sermon, and then quickly depart through the closest exit without making eye contact with anyone on the way out. For us, that's the perfect arrangement. We get the God stuff, but we avoid entanglements with a mass of humanity that we don't really know and don't particularly care about.

This scenario, which many of us live out from week to week, has one slight problem: It isn't according to God's plan. The Bible-thumping, itinerant gospel preachers of yesteryear would call such behavior sin. Unfortunately, that word is falling out of our Christian vocabulary, but let's at least admit that this conduct is a major departure from what Christ had in mind when he told us to love each other just as he loved us.

If we are going to follow Christ's command to love each other, he undoubtedly wants us to begin in our respective local fellowships—our churches—because that's where we find ourselves surrounded by a collection of Christian brothers and sisters to love. We don't have to go looking for a pool of potential candidates. God has conveniently placed them in the nearby seats at church.

⌒

Tragically, many Christian churches are merely collections of acquaintances. The people who attend have little more than a casual familiarity with each other. They aren't close friends, and they certainly don't feel like members of the same family. Most people in these churches are isolated individuals, passing each other with nary a nod in the church lobby. The only time they actually speak to each other is during a forced meet-and-greet moment between worship choruses.

Christians experience a progressive understanding of what a church is. At the most elementary level, they use the word "church" to describe the physical buildings on the property. We go to the church. Our parents told us to be quiet in the church. You can't wear the Hooters T-shirt at church.

As we become a part of what is happening at those buildings, our perception of the term changes from a noun to a verb: Church becomes an activity. We still go to the church (the building), but we also go there to do church. Everything that happens in a worship service (the praying, singing, teaching, and so on) is church. At this level of understanding, all of what we do together as Christians becomes church. So even when you're on a camping trip with the family, you can still have church on Sunday mornings.

But the terminology is best understood when it is internalized. In that context, church is who we are—a loving, caring group of believers in Christ who are committed to him and to each other. We are the church when we love God and love each other because of him. We are a living, breathing organism, and each one of us is vital to the functioning of the whole.

The church is still a pleasant place if we think of it only as a place we go. And it can serve beneficial purposes when we consider it as the things we do. But a spiritual transformation happens when we start thinking of church as being who we are collectively in and through our relationship with Christ. Then Christ becomes more than a picture on the wall or a frequently reoccurring word in our conversation. When we grasp that *we* are the church when we love each other through him, the quantity and quality of our love for each other is what defines us. Imagine the paradigm shift that would occur in many churches if we committed ourselves to really loving each other instead of just associating with each other. Here are four changes we would experience.

1. Our churches would become restful places for us to heal. The world is rough on most of us. We get beaten, battered, and bruised in everyday life. It happens in our finances. It happens in our relationships. And it happens to us emotionally and physically. Most people in our society have no one to turn to for care and comfort in the difficult times of life. But those of us in a local fellowship of believers are able to turn to our church family. We can cry in other believers' arms, be comforted by their sympathy, and be encouraged by their assistance. Figuratively speaking, the church family should be experts at bandaging each other's wounds.

2. Our churches would become safe places to fail. Our culture does not tolerate failure. It ridicules defeat. It labels people who fail as outcasts. But in the church, failure is the one thing we all have in common. We are all sinners, and we have failed to meet God's standard of holiness.[20] And even though we all aspire to "go and sin no more," each of us constantly fails at that too.[21] So our churches should be filled with people who are understanding of each other—not tolerant of sin, but quick to extend grace to each other when we fail, just as all of us have received God's grace.

3. Our churches would become encouraging places to grow. The world applauds winners and has little affection for those who also ran. But in the church, we should be encouraging spiritual growth at whatever rate it occurs. Some will mature spiritually faster than others, but we aren't in a race against the other members of the church family. We are all moving along the path toward knowing God better, so any

forward progress is significant. And if some folks take two steps backward and stumble, we should be cheering them on to stand up and take one step forward once again.

4. Our churches would become challenging places to serve. The world equates people's worth with the prestige or insignificance of their roles. But the church has no small roles. We are all engaged in service to the King. The functions we perform may be different, but we are each participating in work of eternal significance. And ours is no ordinary work; we're engaged in a battle against the dark forces of the spiritual world.[22] We don't fight this battle alone, because we are in the trenches with our Christian brothers and sisters.

But this transformation of our churches won't happen if we simply think of church as a place to go or a thing we do. It will only happen when we realize that the church is who we are when we are loving each other as Christ loved us.

~

If we want to see God more clearly, we need to start looking for Jesus in the faces of our church family. And not just those with whom we are already best friends. We need to extend ourselves to the people at our church who appear to have no best friends or no friends at all. We need to treat those individuals with the love and kindness we would show to Christ himself if he were at our church—because loving them is the same as loving Christ.

> When he finally arrives, blazing in beauty and all his angels with him, the Son of Man will take his place on his glorious throne. Then all the nations will be arranged before him and he will sort the people out, much as a shepherd sorts out sheep and goats, putting sheep to his right and goats to his left.
>
> Then the King will say to those on his right, "Enter, you who

are blessed by my Father! Take what's coming to you in this kingdom. It's been ready for you since the world's foundation. And here's why:

> I was hungry and you fed me,
> I was thirsty and you gave me a drink,
> I was homeless and you gave me a room,
> I was shivering and you gave me clothes,
> I was sick and you stopped to visit,
> I was in prison and you came to me."

Then those "sheep" are going to say, "Master, what are you talking about? When did we ever see you hungry and feed you, thirsty and give you a drink? And when did we ever see you sick or in prison and come to you?" Then the King will say, "I'm telling the solemn truth: Whenever you did one of these things to someone overlooked or ignored, that was me—you did it to me."

Then he will turn to the "goats," the ones on his left, and say, "Get out, worthless goats! You're good for nothing but the fires of hell. And why? Because—

> I was hungry and you gave me no meal,
> I was thirsty and you gave me no drink,
> I was homeless and you gave me no bed,
> I was shivering and you gave me no clothes,
> Sick and in prison, and you never visited."

Then those "goats" are going to say, "Master, what are you talking about? When did we ever see you hungry or thirsty or homeless or shivering or sick or in prison and didn't help?"

He will answer them, "I'm telling the solemn truth: Whenever you failed to do one of these things to someone who was being over-looked or ignored, that was me—you failed to do it to me."[23]

Did you catch his description of himself as "someone who was being overlooked or ignored"? Our churches are filled with people who are being overlooked and ignored. If we start looking at them, we'll see Jesus.

...Because I
Like My Life
Just the
Way It Is

Life isn't perfect, but for most of us, it isn't too bad either. If measured on a scale of one (being the worst) to ten (being the best), most of us would be at five or higher. And compared with the circumstances of most people with whom we share the earth, our lives would score almost ten. Let's admit it—we've got it good. Maybe too good for our own good.

Sure, from time to time we have relationship issues in our marriages, parent-child conflicts, and irritating siblings. The pressures of a job—finding one, keeping one, enduring one, or recovering from losing one—are constant. The bills keep coming every month. And our health...well, we can only take that one day at a time whether we're trying to stay healthy or hoping to get healthy. I don't mean to minimize any of that. But all things considered, we've got it pretty good. We wake up every morning, we eat three (or more) meals each day, and we live in relative comfort and peace. Unlike the residents of Afghanistan and Iraq, most of us aren't dodging bullets and bombs as we walk through our neighborhoods. Unlike millions who live in abject poverty around the world, we are not scrounging for morsels of food. Our lives are warm, full, and relatively happy.

My life has its challenges, but I'm pretty much happy with the way things are. I don't want things to get worse, but I'd be all right if they never got better. I like the physical circumstances of my life just the way it is.

So as I seek to develop the spiritual side of my life—as I desire to have a more passionate faith—and as I search for that abundant life Jesus promised in John 10:10, I do so with fear and trepidation. I want God to give me that abundant life, but I don't want him to mess up the physical circumstances of my life as it is right now. I've got a good thing going, and I'm not sure I want to give it up in exchange for the elusive and mysterious abundant life.

Isn't it ironic? I've received so many earthly blessings from God that now I'm reluctant to lose them in the process of knowing him better. It's more than ironic. It's tragic.

❦

I love hanging out with new Christians. They are excited and passionate about their newfound faith. They are eager to absorb information and insights about Christ and to become his followers. They are on fire about the Lord. If you get them talking about the change they've experienced in their lives, they go on and on about it. You can't shut them up.

On the other end of the spectrum is another group. These are spiritually mature believers who are on the front lines of advancing the kingdom. You can't shut these guys up either. They are hip-deep in ministry, and they want to tell you about the victories they've seen as God has miraculously overcome seemingly insurmountable obstacles. They might be talking about their work in an orphanage in AIDS-ravaged Africa or about sharing Christ and a meal with women who work in the strip clubs in Las Vegas. Maybe they do something as inconspicuous as taking the kids in the church youth group to clean the yards of homes in a neglected part of the city.

I've noticed that both groups, the new believers and the mature believers, have a few things in common. The depth of their spiritual understanding of doctrine and theology may be drastically different, but both groups are passionate about their faith. And the excitement of both groups seems to be connected to the experience of seeing God at work in their lives, because both groups live in the face of constant challenges.

The new believers face challenges that have to do with temptations—temptations to doubt God's existence and his promises, temptations to return to an old lifestyle, temptations to keep their conversion a secret in the face of criticism by skeptical friends and family. Yet the victory that Christ gives them over these temptations reinforces their excitement about him.

The more mature believers often confront challenges that have to do with suffering of some sort—they experience health challenges or financial struggles, their ministries are under some kind of persecution, or circumstances seem stacked against them on a frequently reoccurring basis. Regardless, their faith in Christ is strengthened all the more as they rely on God to supply their every need.

These two groups, polar opposites on the "How long have you been a Christian?" continuum, both seem to experience the abundant life that Christ promised in John 10:10. Whether they have just met Christ or they have been in a relationship with him for decades, they seem to experience his fullness in their everyday lives. This fact tells me two things: First, the abundant life isn't something that necessarily wears off after you have been a Christian for a while. And second, the abundant life isn't a promise that kicks in only after you've been enrolled in the Christianity program for so many years that you qualify for a senior's discount at the church's coffee bar. Experience of the abundant life is unrelated to the length of time that you've been a Christian.

Stuck in the Valley of Complacency

I think I'm like a lot of Christians—stuck somewhere in the middle between those exuberant new Christians and the enthusiastic mature Christians. Those two groups are having mountaintop experiences, but I'm often down in the valley. Way down. Down so low that there is little excitement. But there is also little temptation and little struggle. That's because the valley is permeated with complacency. I'm not alone down here. I've got plenty of company because many Christians are experiencing a mundane life of spiritual complacency.

I'm not sure how we slid into spiritual complacency, but I have a theory. For many of us, the focus of our early Christian years was mistakenly centered on avoiding sin. Our preachers and teachers, the Bible, and the Holy Spirit all reminded us that Christians don't do certain things. We wanted to be good Christians, so we worked diligently on our sin management. Some of us worked on that so much that we didn't focus on developing our relationship with Christ. After all, we thought, once we get our sin under control, we can put our Christian life on autopilot. So while we were striving to control the urges, thoughts, and actions that ensnare us in sin, we were letting our relationship with Christ atrophy. Our sin management techniques grew stronger (or so we thought), but our love for Christ was not fortified.

Satan is no fool when he sees this happening. Sure, he is big on temptation and gleefully watches us stumble into sin. But once we're Christians, he can't snatch us out of the Shepherd's fold.[1] So at that point, enticing us with sin and keeping us from salvation is no longer his primary concern. Instead, he becomes intent in making us useless for kingdom purposes. Simply put, he wants us disengaged from our spiritual passion. If the struggles of temptation keep a new believer walking closely with the Lord, Satan may employ a strategy of backing off on temptation. Let the naive Christians think that they have managed to conquer the sin problem if it causes them to reduce their reliance on God. Get them to a place of complacency in their spiritual lives—a place where they exist as Christians but aren't compelling advertisements for Christianity. I suspect that Satan has no problem with complacent Christians because they are simply no threat to his agenda.

We Christians have been warned about the dangers of sin more than we have been warned about spiritual complacency. Yet the latter can be more destructive than the former. When we're sinning, we usually realize the damage it causes. We are aware that sin disrupts our fellowship with God and causes lots of problems if we continue to let it go unabated. But spiritual complacency is deceptively subtle. It also interrupts our fellowship with God, but we don't readily realize it. And if we don't remedy the situation, we become unconsciously but progressively more calloused to God's influence in our lives.

Preacher and theologian A.W. Tozer recognized the dangers of spiritual complacency when he wrote, "Complacency is the deadly enemy of spiritual progress. The contented soul is the stagnant soul."[2] Tozer also explained why complacency disconnects us from God: "The average Christian is so cold and so contented with his wretched condition that there is no vacuum of desire into which the blessed Spirit can rush in satisfying fullness."[3]

If you've been living in the valley of spiritual complacency, those words are likely to resonate with you. But there is hope. Even if we're mired in complacency, God can pull us out. But the process might be a little frightening.

The Suffering Solution

If we've lost the exuberance we had as new believers, we should look to the example of mature Christians who remain excited about their faith. The difference between them and us usually boils down to an understanding of what constitutes a normal Christian life.

We who struggle with complacency usually think a normal spiritual life is tranquil. For the mature, passionate Christian, however, a normal Christian life commonly includes suffering.

The Bible doesn't beat around the burning bush about this fact: Suffering is a key component of the complete Christian life. Our churches don't put this fact in their slogans or their advertising brochures for Christianity, but Jesus never kept it a secret. He proclaimed it with absolute clarity to his disciples: "In this world you will have trouble."[4]

The first-century Christians didn't need to be told that suffering was a part of their faith. Most of them experienced the harsh reality on a daily basis. Nonetheless, Paul wrote often about it to reinforce the spiritual dimension of what they were enduring:

- "Now if we are children, then we are heirs—heirs of God and co-heirs with Christ, if indeed we share in his sufferings in order that we may also share in his glory."

- "In fact, everyone who wants to live a godly life in Christ Jesus will be persecuted."

- "I want to know Christ and the power of his resurrection and the fellowship of sharing in his sufferings."[5]

And Peter also wrote that suffering was a good thing:

Dear friends, don't be surprised at the fiery trials you are going through, as if something strange were happening to you. Instead, be very glad—for these trials make you partners with Christ in his suffering, so that you will have the wonderful joy of seeing his glory when it is revealed to all the world.[6]

It's one thing for Paul and Peter to say that suffering is beneficial. It's another thing to realize how that can be true.

Learning to See Suffering As God Intends to Use It

We know that suffering may be the natural consequence of our sin (the result of our bad choices) and that God can bring suffering on us as punishment for our sins. But we must not always associate suffering with being at odds with God. To do so will cause us to view suffering only in a negative context. We must begin to see suffering for the purposes God so often uses it—to bring us closer to him. Here are three ways he does that.

1. Sometimes God uses suffering in our lives to help shape our perspective about ourselves. This was certainly the case with Paul, who prior to being a Christian must have been one arrogant son of a Hebrew. Paul readily admits that his thorn in the flesh (which many Bible commentators speculate was a physical infirmity) served the purpose of keeping him humble.

> So to keep me from becoming proud, I was given a thorn in my flesh, a messenger from Satan to torment me and keep me from becoming proud. Three different times I begged the Lord to take it away. Each time he said, "My grace is all you need. My power works best in weakness." So now I am glad to boast about my weaknesses, so that the power of Christ can work through me. That's why I take pleasure in my weaknesses, and in the insults, hardships, persecutions, and troubles that I suffer for Christ. For when I am weak, then I am strong.[7]

2. Sometimes God uses suffering in our lives to help shape our perspective about him. Difficulties cause us to look at God in a new way. We encounter the reality of his abiding presence. We understand his faithfulness. Our theology morphs from mere theory into actual, practical experience. This is what happened to the king of suffering, Job. God allowed the loss of Job's wealth, health, and family. Everything he had was painfully extracted from him. Remember that Job was selected as the target of Satan's challenge because he revered God. So even though he already knew and worshipped God, Job saw God in a new, more meaningful reality as the result of his sufferings. That is the message he conveyed when he prayed to God, "I had only heard about you before, but now I have seen you with my own eyes."[8]

3. Sometimes God uses suffering in our lives to help shape our

perspective about others. If our lives are free from troubles and tribulations (as will be the case when we're spiritually complacent), we might have little sensitivity to the sufferings of others. We might throw them a sympathetic bone from time to time, but we have no real empathy for or with them. We can even become spiritually arrogant about the differences, thinking that their suffering is due to some fault of theirs and believing that we enjoy a preferred life because we are superior to them in some way. Of course, we would never vocalize these opinions, but our indifference toward the poor, the downtrodden, and those who are hurting reveals the attitude in our hearts. To remedy our shortsightedness, God may bring suffering into our lives to teach us how to comfort others.

> God is our merciful Father and the source of all comfort. He comforts us in all our troubles so that we can comfort others. When they are troubled, we will be able to give them the same comfort God has given us. For the more we suffer for Christ, the more God will shower us with his comfort through Christ. Even when we are weighed down with troubles, it is for your comfort and salvation! For when we ourselves are comforted, we will certainly comfort you. Then you can patiently endure the same things we suffer.[9]

These are some of the ways in which God uses suffering in our lives to mature us as believers. Whatever the specific reason may be, the overarching benefit is that suffering draws us closer to him. God knows that the development of our relationship with him is in our ultimate best interest, and he will put us through difficulties—ones that we might otherwise prefer to avoid—to achieve that purpose. The writer to the Hebrews reminds us of the value of this: "For our earthly fathers disciplined us for a few years, doing the best they knew how. But God's discipline is always good for us, so that we might share in his holiness."[10]

Of course, hard times aren't fun. We would prefer not to have to endure them. But the mature Christian understands that the product of hard times is worth the experience: "No discipline is enjoyable while it is happening—it's painful. But afterward there will be a peaceful harvest of right living for those who are trained in this way."[11]

Surviving in Tough Times

We admire Christians who boldly endure sufferings, but our admiration doesn't automatically motivate us to do the same. Our intellectual knowledge of the spiritual benefits of suffering must be bolstered by something more in order for us to move out of our complacency. A reminder of God's sovereignty might help. Nothing ever enters our lives that he doesn't allow, so he not only is aware of suffering but also is capable and eager to equip us for the struggle. We've seen his reminder to Paul: "My grace is all you need. My power works best in weakness."[12]

But ultimately it boils down to a matter of faith. Do we trust that God will bring us through the sufferings he allows in our lives and use them to stoke our spiritual passion? Intellectually, we know that "by his divine power, God has given us everything we need for living a godly life."[13] But we also know that the reality of suffering will burst the serene bubble of our complacent life. Our circumstances will change from tranquil to tumultuous.

But we must not let our fear of suffering cloud our thinking. In the final analysis, we don't doubt God's love, protection, and provision. We don't doubt that he uses suffering for our ultimate benefit. Our trepidation of suffering, at its core, comes from the unknown aspect of what the experience might entail. But that is what faith is all about—entering a situation of unknown circumstances with the confidence that God is in control and that he will use the experience to accomplish his purposes.

We have to choose where to put our focus. Are we going to fix our gaze on the front end, fearfully looking at what the yet-unknown suffering may entail? Or can we look beyond to the resulting outcome of the suffering process—a more passionate faith? The answer lies in whether we're sufficiently disgusted with a complacent faith and ready to trade it for the alternative of an abundant life. It is a question of how badly we want to see God.

⌀

I don't have a paralyzing fear of God, but I am sometimes afraid that his plan for my life will include a significant disruption to my relatively calm and pleasant circumstances. I feel the same way Peter must have felt when Jesus gave him a quick look at what was in store for his future.

> I tell you the truth, when you were young, you were able to do as you liked; you dressed yourself and went wherever you wanted to go. But when you are old, you will stretch out your hands, and others will dress you and take you where you don't want to go.[14]

Most Bible commentators interpret this verse to foreshadow Peter's violent death. In other words, his martyrdom by crucifixion (tradition says he was hung upside down) was what Jesus meant when he said others would take him where he didn't want to go. I don't think the sufferings that God may have in store for me will come anywhere close to a Roman execution, but I am still apprehensive about going down that road. I'm afraid it is a place where I don't want to go.

We lukewarm Christians don't want suffering, but if we're serious about our faith, we know we must not stay mired in our spiritual complacency. If we are going to recommit to living our Christianity in the way God designed it, we must accept the eventuality of suffering as a part of our faith.

The prospect of suffering is not appealing, but a mediocre Christian life should be even more repulsive to us. So if we want to have a fresh and unobstructed view of God, we need to be willing to step out and gratefully receive any difficult challenges that God wants to bring into our lives. We don't need to be praying for suffering, but we ought to expect it.

Getting a Glimpse of God

FIXING OUR FOCUS

The problem is not that we've never seen God or experienced an abundant life. Those things have happened for us in the past, but we got distracted somewhere along the way. We took our eyes off of God, and as his image became more obscured, the abundant life dissipated. We know what life with Christ can be like, and we long to get back on track. We want more of God in our lives.

Maybe that's the problem. We want more of God in us, but the solution might be to put more of ourselves into God. But that means that we cannot remain the central focus of our own lives.

⌒

If we want to see God, we need to get out of the way. We need to stop trying to manipulate our faith into a shape that suits our preferences. Instead, we need to cooperate with God as he transforms our lives according to a biblical pattern for following Christ.

When the Bible encourages us to surrender ourselves to God, we need to surrender everything, not just the aspects of our lives that we can release without disrupting our plans.

Our view of God must change. We must not view him as a divine assistant whose role is to facilitate the life we have planned for ourselves. We need to mentally reverse roles and view ourselves as being engaged in his service and for his pleasure to undertake the work that he wants to accomplish.

We need to stop viewing our lives as *our* lives. Our lives belong to him. And we need to look at the world with his perspective and from his vantage point. We need to view God and his purposes, not our own agendas, as the pivotal point.

The things that we selfishly consider important amount to nothing more than distractions that divert our view of God. The more we remove ourselves from view, the more of God we will see. And when we get God back in our sight, we must keep our focus on him, ignoring the distraction of ourselves.

Let us strip off every weight that slows us down, especially the sin that so easily trips us up. And let us run with endurance the race God has set before us. We do this by keeping our eyes on Jesus, the champion who initiates and perfects our faith.[15]

Notes

Introduction
1. 2 Corinthians 5:21
2. Revelation 3:16

Chapter 1—I Can't See God...Because I Don't Know What He Looks Like
1. This sounds like a verse from the Bible, but it is actually a paraphrase of a commercial for Kellogg's Corn Flakes.
2. Tryptophan is that essential amino acid contained in turkey meat that is often cited as the culprit for post-Thanksgiving dinner lethargy. In actuality, the turkey isn't to blame, but it makes a convenient excuse for a food-induced coma.
3. Deuteronomy 6:5
4. Matthew 13:44
5. Deuteronomy 6:13
6. Deuteronomy 6:18
7. Colossians 1:15
8. Luke 15:3-7; John 10
9. John 8:1-11
10. John 2:13-22
11. Isaiah 6:3
12. Lest you think my son is a rebellious hellion, you should know that his tattoo, about the size of a silver dollar, was in the shape of the Christian fish with a cross in the center.
13. Matthew 22:35-38

14. Romans 12:1

Chapter 2—I Can't See God...Because I Don't Want to Annoy Him with My Prayers

1. See *Why God Won't Go Away: Brain Science and the Biology of Belief* (Ballantine, 2001) or visit www.AndrewNewberg.com.
2. Ecclesiastes 3:11
3. Psalm 139:23
4. Luke 11:5-8
5. Luke 18:2-5
6. Luke 11:9
7. Luke 18:1
8. Oswald Chambers, *The Best from All His Books* (Nelson, 1987), 262.
9. James 5:16
10. Mark 14:32-42; Luke 22:39-46
11. Mark 14:36
12. Mark 14:33-34
13. Luke 22:44
14. Luke 11:10-13
15. James 4:2
16. Adapted from Jeff Brechlin. Original available online at www.phantomranch.net/folkdanc/articles/hokeypokey.htm.
17. Luke 18:10-14
18. Philippians 4:6-7
19. Psalm 27:14

Chapter 3—I Can't See God...Because the Abundant Life Seems like a Myth

1. Matthew 16:13-19
2. Mathew 16:21-23
3. Such as Christine Hassler, *20 Something Manifesto: Quarter-Lifers Speak Out About Who They Are, What They Want, and How to Get It* (New World Library, 2008).
4. John 10:9-10
5. See Matthew 16:24.
6. These phrases come from John 10:10 in the King James Version, the New International Version, The Message, and the Amplified Bible.
7. Isaiah 29:13
8. I put "sexual" in parentheses because that is my way of whispering it.
9. Judges 14–16:3
10. See, for example, Judges 14:19 and 15:14.

11. Judges 13
12. Judges 16:4-14
13. Judges 16:15-21
14. Judges 16:20
15. Acts 2:38-39; Ephesians 1:13
16. Ephesians 5:18
17. See Acts 1:5-8; John 14:15-17; 1 Corinthians 12:1-7.
18. Ephesians 1:14
19. Mark 8:35

Chapter 4—I Can't See God…Because the Bible Seems Irrelevant and Needs More About Me

1. Luke 24:13-32
2. Cambridge Advanced Learner's Dictionary, 2nd ed.
3. For a more helpful perspective, we recommend Mike Erre's excellent book *Death by Church* (Harvest House, 2008).
4. Matthew 16:24-25
5. 1 Samuel 17:46-47
6. 1 Peter 2:2
7. Hebrews 5:11-14
8. 2 Timothy 3:15-17
9. Psalm 119:11,105
10. Psalm 37:4 (NIV)
11. Philippians 4:13
12. Philippians 4:10-14

Chapter 5—I Can't See God…Because I'm Too Concerned with Being Happy

1. See John 17:13-18.
2. Colossians 2:3-4
3. J.P. Moreland and Klaus Issler, *The Lost Virtue of Happiness* (NavPress, 2006).
4. Job 5:17 (KJV)
5. Proverbs 3:13 (KJV)
6. Matthew 5:3-11 (NIV)
7. Matthew 16:24-25
8. Romans 8:28
9. Matthew 11:30
10. Hebrews 3:13 (ASV)

Chapter 6—I Can't See God...Because I Missed the First 37 Years of Eternity

1. The swap of the missionary board for baseball posters was a negotiated event. My mom was opposed to the idea because she believed it was a concession to worldliness, but I convinced her that this was not pagan hero worship if I only put up posters of major leaguers who were Christians. Fortunately for me, she didn't know which players were Christians and which were not. Years later, when Pete Rose was banned from baseball for betting and jailed for tax evasion, she began to suspect that he wasn't a Christian, but by then I had left for college, and she had sold his poster at a garage sale.

2. Romans 5:10

3. 1 Corinthians 1:18

4. Galatians 3:13

5. Ephesians 2:14-16

6. Philippians 2:8

7. Colossians 1:20

8. Hebrews 12:2

9. 1 Peter 2:24

10. 1 John 5:6

11. 1 Corinthians 1:7

12. Philippians 3:20

13. 1 Thessalonians 5:10

14. 2 Timothy 4:8

15. Hebrews 10:25

16. James 5:7

17. 1 Peter 1:3-5,7

18. 1 John 2:28

19. John 14:1-3

20. 1 Corinthians 2:9

21. 1 John 3:2

22. Revelation 21:4,21

23. 1 Peter 3:15 (KJV)

24. Colossians 2:13-14

25. 2 Corinthians 5:17

26. Ephesians 1:13-14

27. Romans 8:2

28. 2 Corinthians 5:17

29. John 17:1-3 (NIV)

30. 1 Kings 11:3

31. See 2 Timothy 3:16-17.
32. Proverbs 5:18
33. Colossians 2:5-7

Chapter 7—I Can't See God...Because My Christianity Is Incognito

1. Matthew 23:27
2. See Matthew 5:13-16.
3. Jim Taylor and Watts Wacker, *The 500-Year Delta* (HarperCollins, 1997).
4. Romans 12:2
5. John 17:20
6. John 17:14-18 (NIV)
7. Daniel 1:4
8. Nehemiah 1:11
9. Matthew 18:19-20
10. George Fielden MacLeod, "Return the Cross to Golgotha," *Focal Point,* January–March 1981.
11. 1 Peter 3:15-16 (NIV)
12. Philippians 4:7
13. 2 Corinthians 10:5

Chapter 8—I Can't See God...Because I'm Hung Up on Finding His Will for My Life

1. Romans 1:20
2. Jeremiah 29:13-14
3. Psalm 143:10; Ephesians 5:17; Colossians 1:9
4. Matthew 10:30
5. Romans 12:33-36
6. Ephesians 5:3-4
7. 2 Peter 3:9
8. 1 John 2:6
9. Colossians 1:9-10
10. See Judges 6:33-40.
11. Esther 4:14
12. Romans 12:2

Chapter 9—I Can't See God...Because I've Lost the Equilibrium of Renewal and Service

1. Mark 3:17
2. Romans 6:23
3. Romans 3:27-28

4. Romans 4:4-5
5. Ephesians 2:8-9
6. James 2:14 (NIV)
7. James 2:26
8. Philippians 3:3-9
9. James 2:17-20
10. Luke 10:38-42
11. Matthew 16:13-16
12. John 11:27
13. Romans 12:13
14. Colossians 3:23 (KJV), which my parents applied out of context a bit. Paul wrote this phrase when he encouraged slaves to work hard for their masters out of reverence for the Lord. I wasn't a slave, but on many Saturday mornings—when my friends were at home sleeping in or watching cartoons—I felt like one.
15. Luke 10:40
16. John 12:1-3 (NIV)
17. Luke 10:41-42
18. Richard Dahlstrom, *O₂: Breathing New Life into Faith* (Harvest House, 2008).

Chapter 10—I Can't See God...Because I Don't Like His Other Children Very Much

1. Matthew 15:1-9
2. Matthew 12:46-50
3. John 13:31–17:26
4. John 13:31-35
5. John 17:20
6. Leviticus 19:18
7. Matthew 5:43-44
8. Luke 10:25-37
9. John 13:34
10. Matthew 22:37-40
11. Romans 8:14-17
12. E.K. Dodds, *Pagan and Christian in an Age of Anxiety* (Cambridge University Press, 1991), 138.
13. Romans 12:9
14. Jerome, *Commentary on Galatians,* at Galatians 6:10
15. 1 John 3:18
16. 1 John 3:17
17. John 15:12-13

18. John 17:20-21
19. John 17:25-26
20. Romans 3:23
21. John 8:11
22. Ephesians 6:12
23. Matthew 25:31-45 (MSG)

Chapter 11—I Can't See God...Because I Like My Life Just the Way It Is

1. See Romans 8:31-39
2. A.W. Tozer, *The Size of the Soul* (Christian Publications, 1992).
3. A.W. Tozer, *Born After Midnight* (Christian Publications, 1986).
4. John 16:33 (NIV)
5. Romans 8:17; 2 Timothy 3:12; Philippians 3:8-11(all NIV)
6. 1 Peter 4:12-13
7. 2 Corinthians 12:7-10
8. Job 42:5
9. 2 Corinthians 1:3-6
10. Hebrews 12:10
11. Hebrews 12:11
12. 2 Corinthians 12:8
13. 2 Peter 1:3
14. John 21:18
15. Hebrews 12:1-2

It's a Harsh,
Crazy,
Beautiful,
Messed Up,
Breathtaking
World...

And People Are Talking About It...

conversant **life**.com

engage your faith